RAILWAY DEVELOPMENT
IN THE OTTOMAN EMPIRE
1856-1914

RAILWAY DEVELOPMENT IN THE OTTOMAN EMPIRE 1856-1914

by

YAQUB N. KARKAR, Ph.D.

VANTAGE PRESS

NEW YORK WASHINGTON HOLLYWOOD

FIRST EDITION

Published by Vantage Press, Inc.
516 West 34th Street, New York, New York 10001

Manufactured in the United States of America

Standard Book No. 533-00267-2

ACKNOWLEDGEMENTS

Writing a book is usually the creation and refinement of many. Thus, I am indebted to a number of professors who have helped me or from whose work I benefited. Prof. J. Batchelor and P. J. Vatikiotis had supervised my original work and have helped me in many respects. The Ford Foundation has contributed to my research. Prof. Roderic H. Davison of Washington University kindly allowed me to quote from his dissertation entitled: *Reform and Westernization in the Ottoman Empire 1856-1876,* published by Princeton University Press in 1963 under the title *Reform in the Ottoman Empire, 1856-1876.* I wish to thank all the additional publishers and individuals who granted me permission to quote from their works. Special thanks are due to three individuals: my uncle Elias M. A. Ṣhanab for his moral support and encouragement, Prof. Linda Ware of the University of Wisconsin Marathon County Center for her editorial work, and Prof. Charles Issawi of Columbia University, an expert on the Ottoman Empire, for recommending my book for publication. Finally, my family deserves much credit for their support and patience.

CONTENTS

BOOK I

BOOK II

BOOK I

BACKGROUND TO RAILWAY DEVELOPMENT IN THE OTTOMAN EMPIRE

CHAPTER I

PHYSICAL FEATURES AND POLITICAL MACHINERY

A. *Introduction*

The eager and often painful efforts by underdeveloped nations to achieve industrialization tend to make this economic objective a commonplace in modern thinking. It comes as something of a shock, then, to realize that a little more than a century ago, the Ottoman Empire had to be jolted into understanding its importance. The economic history of such successfully industrialized countries as Great Britain, France, Germany, Russia, and the United States has been traced in detail, but studies are rare of countries which failed to industrialize. The Ottoman Empire is a significant example of such a country: a survey of its failures and frustrations during the period from 1856 to 1914 can thus offer new perspectives to the problem facing many young nations today.

The choice of 1856 as a starting date and of 1914 as a final one for this discussion is significant, for they are important turning points in the long history of the Ottoman Empire. The first date, 1856, marks the beginning of a new era.[1] A concession was granted to an English company for the purpose of constructing a railway line between Smyrna and Aidin, though construction of this line did not begin until 1863 for financial reasons. During this same year, the Treaty of Paris officially terminated the Crimean War, begun in 1853, between Great Britain, France and Turkey on one side, and Russia on the other; and the Ottoman Empire was brought into the European system of states. The year 1914 is also particularly important: it stands out as the beginning of World War I, in which Turkey was a participant. As a consequence, normal and peaceful activities were interrupted, and the aforementioned railway construction was temporarily halted.

Any year immediately prior to 1856 would have been a good

B4 1856

year to begin this study, except that no railway lines were allowed to be constructed in the Ottoman Empire. The plan to construct railways was not, however, the outcome of a simple and impulsive decision, nor even a development of that year alone. It had been developing in the minds of those concerned for many years. The first railway project was probably considered as early as 1836,[2] at about the same time that railway development was beginning in the United States; however, time was needed for the study of such projects. History, although often divided into periods for convenience of exposition, is obviously a continuous process. Therefore, although we have chosen the period 1856-1914 for a case study of the influence of railway construction upon economic development, it is obvious that the reactions to the impact of railways had their beginnings in institutions evolved much earlier and that consequences continued to emerge long thereafter.

Dating back to the occupation of Constantinople by the Ottomans in 1453, the House of Osman continued through war to extend its rule over adjacent territories. Although the decline of the Ottoman Empire may have started with the destruction of the Turkish fleet at Lepanto in 1571, or with the Treaty of Carlowitz in 1699,[3] some writers place greater emphasis on the year 1774. During this year, the Treaty of Kuchuk Kainarja was negotiated, in which Azow and a part of the Crimea were lost to Tzarist Russia, thus giving her the right of navigation in the Black Sea and the Sea of Azow.[4]

The process of disintegration, due to internal as well as external factors, proceeded at a slow pace until the final blow of World War I. Thanks to the British policy initiated by Palmerston, British Foreign Minister in the 1830's, of maintaining the integrity of the Ottoman Empire, this process was retarded during the nineteenth century. But then, it could wait no longer.

> The signature of the Peace Treaty of Lausanne on 24 July, 1923, marked the close of that epoch in the external history of Turkey which began with the signature of the Peace Treaty of Kuchuk Kainarja on 21 July, 1774. During the intervening century-and-a-half the political map of the Near East had changed beyond recognition. Where formerly there had been one great empire, embracing many people,

there were now a dozen independent sovereign states, each of which was identified with some single Near Eastern nationality.[5]

Estimated at one-sixth of the pre-World War I Ottoman Empire, the modern Republic of Turkey now comprises about 294,416 square miles of territory located almost completely in the Anatolian Peninsula.[6]

> Turkey in Asia means the Asiatic dominions of the Ottoman or Osmanli Turks, who are a minority only of the Turks in Asia, are not of pure extraction, and are associated with a popular majority not Turkish at all. The north-western third of their dominions is the only part which is generally Turkish in feeling. The southern half, almost entirely Arab, identifies itself very imperfectly with Osmanli tradition and hope.[7]

> Turkey in Europe comprises the vilayets of Adrianople and Chatalja, together with about one-third of that of Constantinople, the remainder being on the Asiatic side of the Bosphorus.[8]

An earlier division, by Michelsen, breaks the Ottoman Empire into three sections: The European (Rumli), the Asiatic (Anadulu) and the African (Garb) territories. In 1856, Turkey still had some jurisdiction over her African possessions.[9]

Regardless of these convenient geographical divisions, Ottoman society deviated from the traditional society prevalent in the West not only in the degree of its development but also in its social structure, which thwarted particularly the entrepreneur and militated against industrial development.[10] The institutional attitudes, mores, customs, methods of organization and laws that formed a climate of opinion, together with the social structure within the country, all checkmated reform and progress. The lack of financial capital, the burden of the public debt, the prevalent totalitarian rule, the degree of industrial and technical backwardness and lack of security (to be discussed later) were largely responsible for the empire's backwardness.

Thus, it will be maintained throughout this discussion that in spite of large improvements in the means of communication, the Ottoman Empire remained largely pre-industrial, that is, in the "traditional stage," up to 1914. Though it is true that there were manifestations of the "preconditions for take-off," those were superficial, hardly potent enough to alter the situation and sustain a drive.

> ... the creation of preconditions for take-off required fundamental changes in a well-established traditional society, changes which touched and substantially altered the social structure and political system as well as techniques of production.[11]

Thus the Ottoman Empire never experienced industrialization as it was known in the West. What construction of railways there was was limited in scope and extended over small distances without concomitant changes of significance in roads, ports or industry.

Since our attention will be devoted to the study of the development of railways in the Ottoman Empire and their impact upon the Ottoman economy, several questions need to be answered. We must consider the non-economic as well as the economic reasons for railway development. The impact of any such change in the amount of investment is bound to have widespread consequences: first, the immediate results for suppliers of the factors of production, generated by the investment in the construction process itself; second, the effects of changes in construction or financial techniques whose effects radiate to other aspects of the economy; and finally, once operations begin, their effect upon the size and structure of markets. All three must be examined.

Important questions are thus posed. Did investment in railways really lead to regional specialization, to industrial development, to the rise of new towns, to greater agricultural production, employment, and income? Did it result in population growth, higher standards of living, in fact? What about the formation of guilds or unions, the promulgation of new laws, and the alterations in the social, economic and political climate to adjust to the changes? Were they successful? Did railway growth deter insurrections and avoid wars, or cause further difficulties? Was the economic situation generally strengthened at home and abroad, or weakened? All these questions have to be considered.

Although the task ahead has been hampered by lack of accurate statistical data and marred by deficiencies in source material, the pertinent questions raised must be answered.[12] Two approaches will be used. The first one deals primarily with a set of facts about the Ottoman Empire itself,[13] gathered, evaluated and presented in a systematic manner. Some of the indirect ramifications of these facts should also be considered. The second approach is a study of the differences between what resulted in the Ottoman Empire as a consequence of railway development, and what had taken place in other countries at that time. Comparing and contrasting railway development in the Ottoman economy with similar developments in a selected group of countries—Great Britain, the United States, and, to a lesser extent, Tzarist Russia—can offer a significantly clearer perspective on the development undertaken.

Some of the questions raised earlier may be adequately dealt with in the first book, which emphasizes the institutional setting then in existence in the Ottoman Empire. Some objection may be raised with regards to the major stress laid on the background to railway development, since it may be said that it does not require much time or space to see the obvious. Nonetheless, the predominant influence of the institutional background, in terms of the political, economic, and social setting in which the economy had flourished, explains much of what happened both then and later. One of the conclusions to be drawn may be that, if these institutional trammels had been loosened earlier, economic development would certainly have taken a different and better course.

B. *Geography and Population*

The Ottoman Empire in 1856 included parts of Europe (Rumli), of Asia (Anadulu) and of Africa (Garb), the islands of Crete, Cyprus and the Aegean Sea, and embraced an area roughly equal to 913,000 square miles.[14] Its possessions in Europe extended as far North as the Pruth, the Carpathians, the Danube and the Save rivers, with Serbia, Moldavia, Wallachia and Greece being excepted. In Asia, the Eastern Ottoman border ran from the Black Sea northeast of Kars to Russian Georgia. Turning to the South, it reached between the lakes of Van and Urmia to the Persian Gulf. In Arabia proper, Ottoman possessions included a half moon area north of the central desert and a strip on the western coast extending to Mecca and Medina. In North Africa, Tripoli was the only integral part of the Empire; Tunis and Egypt were autonomous tributaries.[15]

> Turkey is a country having three thousand miles of coast still remaining, a territory of five hundred thousand square miles, under the happiest climate, possessed of the richest soil, raising every variety of produce, having unrivalled facilities of transport, abounding in forests and mines, opening innumerable communications with countries further to the East.[16]

This is a vivid description, designed to capture the minds and hearts of the British people at that time; nevertheless it is a reasonable summing-up of the situation.

A later and more objective observer, Frank Edgar Bailey, elaborates with a lengthy description of the fine ports that studded those three thousand miles of coast line at the time of the Crimean War. The major ports include Constantinople, Smyrna, Salonica, Beirut, Alexandretta, Eons (part of Adrianople), Galacz at the mouth of the Danube, Trebizond and Scutari. He also gives a detailed account of the export and import trading taking place in these ports, with particular attention devoted to Turkish-British commercial relations between 1823 and 1853.

> Constantinople possessed a deep, sheltered harbor with anchorage for as many as twelve hundred ships. While more ships entered and cleared in the Golden Horn than in any other port of the empire, Constantinople was by no means the most important commercial city of the empire. Because of its location many ships made it a port of call on their way to and from the Black Sea ports; also, it should be noted that the great majority of the vessels clearing at Constantinople were small coastwise vessels under Greek command.[17]

More important than Constantinople as a trading center in the first half of the nineteenth century was Smyrna in Asia Minor; in fact Smyrna might be called the first commercial city of the Near East. While the population of Smyrna was not to be compared with that of Constantinople, its well protected harbor and its connections with the interior gave it an advantage over the Turkish capital.[18]

Smyrna was located in the center of one of the most fertile districts of Asia Minor as well as on a direct line between the European markets and the distant East, and had been for many years the embarkation point for caravans en route to Syria, Bagdad, and Persia. . . . Symrna handled more foreign produce than any other port of the empire.[19]

One of the most valuable exports from this port was manufactured silk, which was brought by caravan from Brusa, the Lyons of Turkey, some 200 miles distant. In 1839, for example, more than £15,000 worth of made-up silk was sent to England alone.[20]

A vivid description of other important ports and towns, including Beirut (with a population of about 10,000 in the 1830's), Alexandretta (Scanderoun), Salonica, Adrianople, Galacz, Trebizond and others, is also given. Salonica is described as an important terminal for overland trade from central Europe, an anchor point for the distribution of British goods to Macedonia and to the borders of Hungary. Adrianople (population about 100,000) was not a British trade center because of its inland position in the province of Roumelia. And, finally, Trebizond is described as

located in northern and eastern portion of Asia Minor. From Persia and Afghanistan the caravans brought carpets, shawls, and silks which the 'rayahs' exchanged with British and foreign merchants for cottons, woolens, western silk, glass and sugar. Some tobacco, nuts, fruits and other soil products were also exported from this region, but the transit trade was really more important in this part.[21]

Unfortunately, the importance of this large set of picturesque ports, which accommodated hundreds of ships, was undermined by the lack of an adequate internal means of communication. There were no natural waterways such as rivers and lakes which could connect these ports with the interior. No canals were dug. Even good roads did not exist. Consequently, cheap transportation was impossible. Reliance was heavy upon beasts of burden: the camel, the mule, the horse and the donkey moved slowly on rugged and often mountainous paths. The processes of loading, transporting and unloading were lengthy and most of all, expensive. The high cost, however, did not obstruct the flow of merchandise to and from these ports, but merely limited it to luxury items. In those days, luxury items were those goods in high demand and whose prices were high in proportion to their bulk. Spices and silks are such examples.

With regard to population, accurate censuses were impossible to undertake, for

> In each community the attempt was made to report a population smaller than the true total in order to diminish the tax burden and to escape the heavy incidence of military service. The census method was generally a count of houses and multiplication by the estimated average number of a family under one roof.[22]

This of course failed to account for the nomadic tribes and gypsies that roamed around the Empire.

After the Balkan War of 1912-1913, the total population in the Ottoman Empire was estimated at 21,273,900, residing in an area of 710,224 square miles, the average being about 30 persons to the square mile.

These figures, and the statistical data presented in the Appendix, are based on estimates which, inaccurate as they are, provide an idea of the area held by the Ottoman Empire and the population which occupied it. Among other things, the impact of wars and loss of territory was noticeable in the continued decrease in the population and area figures up to 1914. With the crystallization of new Turkey, the area which emerged was 438,750 square miles, holding a population of 8 million, or an average of 18.2 persons to the square mile.

C. *Political Administration*

Michelsen gives a succinct description of the Ottoman Government around 1856, which, with some exceptions, particularly those brought about by the Vilayet Law of November, 1864, continued to be the same throughout the period under discussion.

> The Turkish Empire is an absolute monarchy, at the head of which stands the monarch (Padishah). He is, however, not above, but under the law. He is the executive power of that law, which he may modify, but never abrogate. The supreme state's laws are the *Koran*, whose ordinances to statutes are immutable. They may be supplied or modified by the decrees (Kanuns) of the sultans, but these decrees are of a temporary character, and may in turn be abrogated at any time. The insufficiency of the law is supplied by use and custom (Adet, Imsal). The throne descends to the eldest male member of the dynasty, who must be born upon the throne. All children, male and female, thus born, bear the title of sultan; but no one besides. In modern diplomacy, the sultan is addressed as 'his imperial majesty.'[23]
>
> The sultan exercises his power through the grand-vizier (Sadr Azam), who is addressed 'highness,' and comprises in himself the highest and last tribunals of all the civil and miiltary departments. Equal to him in rank stands the Sheik-ul-Islam (commonly, though wrongly, called mufti), whose proper function is the interpretation of the law. His department somewhat resembles that of the continental ministers of justice and worship. He has the same pay as the grand-vizier, and also bears the title of 'highness.'[24]
>
> The whole Ottoman Empire is divided into Eyalets, at the head of which stands a *Vali* (Viceroy), or Mutessarif (Governor General). Every *Eyalet* is again subdivided into Livas, governed by a *Kaimakam* (Sub, or Deputy-Governor), or Muhassil (Prefect). The *Liva* is again divided into *Kazas* (districts), and the latter again into *Nahyes* (communities or villages).[25]

Prior to the promulgation of the Vilayet Law of 1864, the 1852 firman gave the *valis* greater power over police, over the punishment of crime, over the provincial treasurer and over the subordinate political units. Besides,

> The law of the Vilayets, of 1864, had intended to grant to the provinces a large measure of self-government, in which both Moslems and Christians were to participate. In reality, however, the government of the Empire was centralized more than ever in the Sultan's hands. In effect this meant that opportunities were multiplied at Constantinople to exercise influence over the Sultan.[26]

The new law reduced the number of *eyalets* from thirty to twenty-seven.

> Each vilayet was divided into a number of *sanjaks* sometimes called *livas,* (a subdivision of the old eyalet), each *sanjak* into *Kazas,* and each *Kaza* into communes and small hamlets known as nahiyas.[27]

Consequently, the vilayet was an enlarged eyalet with a new administrative system with subdivisions. The whole divisional hierarchy was modelled after the French *Departement* and its subdivisions.[28] While this was reasonable in principle, the lack of properly trained personnel and an enlightened and patriotic ministry to run the vilayets honestly decreased the effectiveness of the Vilayet Law.[29]

When Sultan Abdul Hamid II came upon the throne of Turkey in 1876, rigidities in the administrative structure again returned, as power became more centralized than ever in the hands of the Sultan.

> The new Sultan (Abdul Hamid), though bitterly hostile to liberal or constitutional ideas, was by no means entirely opposed to reform and Westernization in which, judiciously selected and applied, he saw the means of reinforcing both the Ottoman Empire and his own position in it. Abdulhamid was far from being blind, uncompromising, complete reactionary of the historical legend; on the contrary, he was a willing and active modernizer, the true heir of Sultan Ab-

> dulaziz and the statesmen of the 'Tanzimat,' against whose autocratic reformism the Young Ottomans had levelled the first Turkish liberal critique of despotic government.[30]

After the Young Turkish Revolution of 1908, and up to World War I, very few changes took place. Furthermore, the span of time between 1908 and the intervention of World War I was short, and the troubled situation in which Turkey then found herself frustrated any progressive changes that may have been on the minds of the new ruling group.

D. *Wars and Insurrections*

Although the century following the Napoleonic Wars is referred to as a period of relative peace in the world, such a characterization does not appear to apply to the Ottoman Empire. During this time, as Birge indicates,[31] a number of belligerent events had taken place. The reason why these different wars and rebellions were significant is simple: They were costly and disastrous to the Ottoman economy. It is not necessary to explore fully the extent of the resultant costs and destruction. Suffice it to say that extensive damages to Turkey were the unfortunate consequences: the loss of territory, drain on human and natural resources, payments of indemnity, expenditures on arms and armaments, loss of tribute, and the attention of both the government and the people focussed upon the preceding. External consequences also followed: Foreign Powers began to intervene in the affairs of Turkey. The resulting insecurity had, for a variety of reasons, various effects on investment and development. One specific and particularly noticeable effect was obvious, however, in these catastrophes. They had an immense impact on the development of railway transportation.

The following, for example, is a chronological list of wars, insurrections, and losses in the 19th and in the early 20th centuries that were significant:[32]

1804-1817 Serbian War of Independence
1808 Loss of Egypt to Mehemet Ali
1821-1829 Greek War of Independence
1826 Destruction of the Janissaries

Photo OP

1828	Russo-Turkish War[33]
1830	France's acquisition of its original foothold in Algeria[34]
1831-1833	Conquest of Syria and invasion of Anatolia by Mehemet Ali[35]
1839-1841	Settlement between Mehemet Ali and the Sultan at the hands of Foreign Powers
1854-1956	Crimean War
1860	Insurrection in Lebanon
1862	Insurrection in Herzegovina
1866-1877	Balkan States in revolt
1875-1876	Bulgarian and Serbian insurrection
1878	British establishment of right to occupy and administer Cyprus
1881	French protectorate established over Tunis
1882	British occupation of Egypt
1897	Turkey declared war on Greece
1903	Bulgarian uprising repressed ruthlessly
1908	Young Turk revolt, Austria's annexation of Bosnia-Herzegovina and Bulgaria's declaration of independence
1911-1912	Turco-Italian war and Turkish cession of Tripoli-Benghazi
1912-1913	The Balkan Wars and loss of Ottoman territory west of Adrianople
1914-1918	The Great War: First World War, and Turkey's intervention on 28 October 1914

The long list above includes only the major wars and insurrections. To make it more comprehensive, one would have to add the many minor revolts and uprisings. The Armenian massacres, for instance, would head such a new list.

E. *Reforms*

Reforms in the Ottoman Empire in the nineteenth and early twentieth centuries were too many and varied to be treated in this discussion adequately. A major classification of reforms with endless subclassifications (for example, of needed, proposed, and actually carried out, of adequate and inadequate, of social, political, military and economic) may be necessary before any significant results can be obtained. Thus a general survey will have to suffice to portray some pertinent aspects of Ottoman reform ambitions and results.

The first in a series of important reforms executed in the nineteenth century was the destruction of the Janissaries in 1826.[36] These had, for many generations, formed an organization of political intrigue that ruled and actually thwarted the course of progress in the empire.

> For almost twenty years the Janissaries had obstructed every reform act on the part of the Sultan, especially those which partook of Westernization; more than once they had dictated policies to the ruler, all of which was anathema to an autocrat like Mahmoud II. The failure of the Janissaries to suppress the rebellious Greeks, together with the threatening attitude of Russia in 1825-26 undermined what little faith many Turks still had in the traditional bodyguard. Some of the most devoted supporters of the Janissaries, especially the 'ulema,'[37] rallied to Mahmoud as the head of the state when his future was thus threatened.[38]

Thus, according to Bailey, the destruction of the Janissaries was not only a significant step on the part of the Sultan, but also a logical one, since their presence had stood in the way of Turkish reform. Besides, many a Sultan had been overthrown at their hands. With their destruction, however, ". . . no social corps was left in the body politic to counterbalance the power and the influence of the bureaucrats of the Porte."[39] In addition, the corps that had performed the function of expressing popular grievances was not replaced, though an attempt was made to replace this vacuum with the rising, educated, young bureaucrats, a new power elite called the Young Ottomans (a subject comprehensively explored by Mardin).[40]

Having administered a mortal blow to the Janissaries, Mahmud then turned his attention to their accomplices, the Ulema. The Ulema (Kadis, Muftis, etc.) were members of the Religious Institution headed by Sheikul-Islam, an appointee of the Sultan with the approval of the Ulema. This body comprised the clergy and the chief functionaries of the law. Since the reign of Suleiman the Magnificent of the early 16th century up to 1826, this aristocratic institution enjoyed supreme control of law, justice, religion and education. The Ulema paid no taxes. Their property was hereditary within their families and not liable to arbitrary confiscation. Their person was sacred. Above all, they received vast independent revenues from the Evkaf (Vakuf, or pious foundations) and wielded much economic power.

In order to bring this religious hierarchy under closer state supervision, the first step undertaken by Mahmud II was to deprive the Ulema of a major source of economic power. He created a Directorate (later, a Ministry) of Evkaf which controlled and disposed of these religious foundation and supervised the collection and administering of their revenues. The upkeep of religious buildings, salaries of religious personnel, and funds for other pious purposes were now handled by the new Directorate instead of by the Ulema.

Mahmud's initial step in this direction was limited but potent. For, by relegating the control of Evkafs and their revenues to a Directorate, he initiated a process that weakened considerably the economic power of the Ulema. His attempts to divert Evkaf revenues to state purposes were carried on by his successors, and as time went by, more drastic measures against the Ulemas reduced them gradually to minor civil servants. But it was not until 1924 that the office of Sheikul-Islam was abolished and the old theological seminaries closed.

> The appointment of teachers and control of schools and colleges was later transferred to a Ministry of Education; the appointment of judges and the administration of the law to a Ministry of Justice; and in time even the drafting of 'fetvas' was entrusted to a committee of legal specialists in the Chief Mufti's office under the Fetva Emin. The Chief Mufti himself became a government office-holder, with some consultative and advisory functions, and with only such effective influence as his own personal character could win for him.[41]

Both the Ulema and the Janissaries had cooperated in past centuries to depose and enthrone Sultans; they had controlled the Porte and were obviously influential in shaping the destiny of the Ottoman Empire. It was not really an act of vengeance that Mahmud attempted in weakening the power of the Ulema, as it was a continuation of a master design to remove all opposition and centralize authority in his person. This, then, was not really a liberal reform intended to create a liberal community, but actually a change towards greater centralization of power. For as power shifted to the Porte, the Sultan and his ministers could carry out unopposed any policies they chose.

Once the Janissaries were eliminated and the Ulema enfeebled, the internal struggle shifted to a new arena: the Sublime Porte. For here, at the seat of the government, the bureaucratic machinery took on new life. It became more powerful in influencing the Sultan. Its members, who were ministers in the employ of the government, began more intensive machinations, and not without the support of foreign nations.

For the sake of simplicity, two major groups in this bureaucracy may be pointed out. The first group, liberals who had acquired Western teachings and ideologies, began pressing for changes in the direction of liberal reforms. The second group, the conservatives, proceeded on a traditional path, attempting to maintain the empire within the framework of Islamic society. In both instances, those who disagreed with predominant policies were only a few individuals and not an organized group or party. However, their influence in affecting the destiny of the Ottoman Empire should not be underestimated.

Naturally, the liberal group found sympathy with the minorities in the empire and received support from the West. The conservative groups had the backing of the masses and the Ulema. A study of the history of the Ottoman Empire until World War I shows that the liberals continued to gain ground. Even under Sultan Abdul Hamid, who was bitterly opposed to liberal and constitutional ideas, reforms and Westernization were undertaken in the belief they would strengthen the Ottoman Empire and thus entrench his position in it.

The fight for power continued even after the deposition of Abdul Hamid in 1908. The annexation of Bosnia-Herzegovina by Austria in the same year, the Turco-Italian War of 1911, the Balkan War of 1912-1913 and the beginning of World War I, all occurring within a period of six years, gave the Young Turks no breathing spell for following any consistent policy of rulership or reform.

Other reforms carried on by Mahmud II included the continued modernization of the military. After the elimination of the Janissaries, the army came under the direct command of the Sultan. The new army was at the Sultan's beck and call; for in his surge for centralized authority, Mahmud needed a strong and rejuvenated force to support his bid. He also sought to have an efficient civil service, to centralize his authority by putting an end to the semi-independent feudal vassals, and to regulate the *dervishes* (members of a secret Muslim order).

Mahmud's efforts were not without some success, despite the exacting demands of wars and rebellions that plagued him during the last years of his reign.[42] His success was greatest in Rumelia and Anatolia, and he initiated a series of reforms which were carried out by his successors. But he failed in Egypt and the Morea (Greece), and reforms of equal importance were badly needed in the administration of the economy and in the social structure. But these had to wait.[43]

While further reforms were carried out at the behest and initiative of later Turkish Sultans, the Western Powers, particularly Britain, began to show interest in the Turkish reform movement. In fact,

> Britain did not fully awaken to the importance of the Ottoman Empire's geographical, political, and economic position in Europe until 1838 when Russia threatened England's position in the Near East by signing with Turkey the Treaty of Unkiar Skelessi.[44]

For, as will be considered shortly, Britain began to implement two objectives with regards to the Ottoman Empire: strengthen the Empire from within, and help it maintain its integrity in case of foreign attack, (possible at the time from Russia and Mohammed Ali).

> Fear of Russia was not the only reason, however, which caused Palmerston to make the Near East an integral part of his foreign policy during the next two decades, i.e., be-

tween 1833 and 1853. British policy during the 19th century was motivated by a variety of influences, political, religious, humanitarian, and last by no means least, economic. The need of new outlets for the increased production of the factories at home was always a driving force in the policy pursued by the Foreign Office. If Turkey was to be free and independent, she must receive sympathetic support from some other power than Russia; an encouragement of the reform movement already in progress was one of the best methods of undermining Russia's influence and thereby making the Porte self-sufficient. Moreover, a strong Turkey would insure an outlet for British produce as well as a source of supply for certain useful raw materials.[45]

The line of reasoning followed by the British advice in the second quarter of the nineteenth century rested on a sound basis. The logic of reform stemmed from the British liberal philosophy of the period and from its experience of many years. The theoretical and practical knowledge of this philosophy found its fullest expression in the Liberal Movement.

> The essence of the Liberal Movement was representative government. It was based on a system of majority rule and individual rights which, in a manner not realised by its first exponents, could ultimately be used for ends as far-reaching as those of the most violent revolutionaries.[46]

As thus tersely theorized, with Palmerston as Foreign Secretary, Britain sought to strengthen the empire from within by encouraging liberal reforms whose purpose was to allow for greater individual liberties, particularly for the minorities, and to create social cohesion within the communities. Though this aim had the additional purpose of maintaining the integrity of the Ottoman Empire, this second objective could in theory, or in principle have been enforced without resort to internal reform. However, both of these objectives, as pursued by Britain, were felt to be intertwined. Reforms in the economic, political, social and military spheres were long overdue. If these reforms were guided by democratic principles and founded on the equality of her people, it was believed that Turkey would eventually be strengthened and capable of resisting Russian advances. These advances towards the Mediterranean could only mean danger to British interests in that part of the world and in India. Therefore, it was to the advantage of Britain to keep Russia in check, and this she tried to do in concert with other European nations. Furthermore, it was held that the disintegration of the Ottoman Empire could bring about war amongst the European nations—a war that none of the Powers desired.

Undoubtedly, with the presence of the *millet* system,[47] no major reform could be successfully carried out if it did not have for its principal aim the creation of a cohesive and flexible unity among the Greeks, the Armenians, the Jews, the Franks and the Muslim majority. With all groups cooperating toward a common national goal, other reforms could be more feasible.

However, any process of social assimilation required a long time to produce results. Since the components of this process were antagonistic from the start, there was no telling how long it would have taken for the different structures within Turkey to crumble and a new one to emerge. Most powerful of all were the deep-rooted emotional barriers founded on long-standing traditions of hatred, implemented by ignorance, illiteracy, prejudice, and outright fear. Without literacy, intermarriages, the acceptance of new social values, there was no hope for constructive changes. Therefore, any reforms by the Western Powers, though proposed with good intentions, depended for their effectiveness on long-run assumptions of the greatest magnitude. Although, at first glance, these reforms did not appear to be superficial to a foreign observer, they had little chance of success. Neither the officials of the Government (with the exception of a few individuals, such as Midhat and Ali Pasha), nor the Muslim masses which constituted the bulk of the Ottoman subjects and were deeply entrenched in their traditions, were willing to accept or to adopt the proposed reforms.[48] But in spite of the seemingly insurmountable obstacles, the early reforms did help to pave the way for individual rights and liberties.

Continued efforts at reform finally resulted in two major *Hattis* (edicts): the *Hatti Sherif of Gulhane*,[49] issued by Sultan Abdul Mejid, under the influence of Reshid Pasha, on November 3, 1839 and the *Hatti Humayun* of February 10, 1856.[50] In essence, the former was a declaration of principles which sought to provide new institutions for the public welfare.

> These institutions must be principally carried out under three heads, which are: 1. The guarantees ensuring to our subjects perfect security for life, honour and fortune. 2. A regular system of assessing and levying taxes. 3. An equally regular system for the levy of troops and the duration of their services.[51]

A deeper consideration of the *Hatti Sherif of Gulhane* evokes the following:

> The proclamation read in the part of Gulhane, in which the promise to respect 'life, honor, and property' held such a prominent place, was not really, as many European's wishful thinking would have had it, a fundamental statement of individual liberties. The 'hatt' was the equivalent of a European constitutional charter only in so far as it promised that henceforth, in the Ottoman Empire, government would be based on principles which eliminated arbitrary rule, but it was only incidentally a "bill of right.'[52]

Interpreted in a different light, which may be considered secondary, the particular question arose: Whose "life, property and honor" did the *Hatti Sherif of Gulhane* protect? The answer is that

> Close study reveals that Mustafa Reshid Pasha had in mind to make the Ottoman state officials benefit from the protection of organic laws which the sultan himself would pledge to observe.[53]

No matter which interpretation is accepted, the decade that followed the enunciation of the *Hatti of Gulhane* witnessed the adoption of several measures which helped establish a modern centralized administration, an assembly of notables, provincial councils, mixed tribunals, and technical schools.

The second, the *Hatti-Humayun,* contained promises of equality and security. The first paragraph reads:

> The guarantees promised on our part by the Hatti-Humayun of Gulhane, and in conformity with the Tanzimat, to all the subjects of my Empire, without distinction to classes or or of religion, for the security of their persons and property and the preservation of their honour, are to-day confirmed and consolidated, and efficacious measures shall be taken in order that they may have their full and entire effect.[54]

One important promise in this *Hatti* has to do with ownership of property.

> As the laws regulating the purchase, sale, and disposal of real property are common to all the subjects of my Empire, it shall be lawful for foreigners to possess landed property in my dominions, conforming themselves to the laws and police regulations, and bearing the same charges as the native inhabitants, and after arrangements have been come to with Foreign Powers.[55]

Further promises with regards to equality of taxes, works of public utility, the budget, the formation of financial institutions, and the *millet* system were made.[56]

Broadly interpreted, these reforms, which constituted the core of the Tanzimat (reforms of 1839 to 1876), were favorable to the Christian population and were steps towards equality, fusion and social assimilation in general.

> In general, the gearing of Turkish reform to the wishes of the Christian populations of the empire made reform something lopsided in which the Moslem populations had no share. Yet reforms were as much needed to ease the lot of the Moslem-Ottomans as they were to make first-class citizens of the Christians.[57]

Commenting on these reforms, Emin states:

> The reforms, however, hardly constituted a real adjustment to new conditions. They were mostly dictated by the pressure of the moment and the instinct of self-preservation.[58]

The apparent efficacy of these reforms is further testified to in this summary:

> Turkey had, by virtue of the Tanzimat, obtained admission to the family of European nations, but she had failed to make good; and Europe had abandoned the doctrine of preservation of the integrity of the Ottoman Dominions.[59]

Perhaps it is too one-sided an argument to put the whole blame on Turkey. The reform movement and the maintenance of the integrity of the Ottoman Empire could be, in fact, treated as two completely different objectives, though Britain wished to treat them jointly, in the belief that a strong democratic state could, in the long run, form a bulwark against Russian designs as well as evoke the sympathy of the Western European Powers in case those Russian designs were implemented. But if the integrity of the Ottoman Empire had to be maintained, then reforms probably had to be set aside. The pretext that the success of reforms should determine whether or not the Western Powers would come to the defense of Turkey was not fully justifiable.

Finally,

> The rock upon which these schemes of reform, like their precursors, were shipwrecked was the inability of the Turco-Moslem, who dominated by the sword, to accord equality before the law or in his administration to the subject Christian and non-Turk races, who were potentially his superiors in culture, economics, and modern progress. He felt that equality meant the eventual submersion of his dominant militarist caste; and though he partially, if reluctantly, admitted his backwardness and the necessity of progress, he was determined not to give an equal opportunity to his subject races and creeds.
>
> Hence, although the Crimean War gained Turkey a respite of 20 years, no adequate improvement was registered during that period.[60]

Needless to say, the abrogation of the Midhat Constitution, which had declared all Ottoman subjects equal before the law, by Sultan Abdul Hamid in 1877, only a year after its promulgation, dampened all hopes for a democratic regime so long as the Sultan reigned.[61] With the deposition of Abdul Hamid in 1908, promises of liberal reforms by the Young Turks met with internal resistance, particularly with disagreement amongst the new rulers, and with external pressures resulting from the several wars in which Turkey was involved, and no significant progress could be achieved.

CHAPTER II

SOCIAL AND RELIGIOUS FACTORS

A. *Religion and State*

The traditional Islamic state was in theory and in the popular conception a theocracy, in which God was the sole legitimate source of both power and law, and the sovereign His vice-regent on earth. The faith and social order. The same Holy Law, coming from the same source and administered through the same juricature, as ritual and doctrinal rules. The sovereign was the supreme embodiment of the Holy Law, maintained by it, and maintaining it. The ulema were its authorized defenders and exponents.[1]

Thus, in Turkey, which may be identified as a Muslim state, the economic, social, political and other structures were founded upon religious laws, primarily those of the Sheri'at (the holy law of Islam, or the unchangeable God-given law) as interpreted by the religious institution. These laws were supplemented by various state laws (the *'Urfa* including *Kanuns, firmans, hattis,* etc.), which allegedly did not violate the Sacred Law.[2]

Although their power had been gradually weakening since 1826, the hold of the Ulema on the masses remained very strong. They opposed the Tanzimat and any liberal reforms imported from the West. For example, in 1841, a new code was introduced to the High Council. Based on French commercial law, it dealt with partnerships, bankruptcies, and bills of exchange. The Ulema opposed it on the grounds that it was not in conformity with the Sacred Law. As long as the Ulema were in charge of education and interpreted narrowly the religious laws *vis-à-vis* changing conditions, their grip on the public mind remained firm. In consequence, the public persisted in its stand against liberal reforms. But as the state gradually took over the system of education, the influence of the Ulema on the younger generations began to decline and the public attitude towards social change became more favorable.[3]

In the West, as the feudal institutions crumbled with the Protestant Reformation, so did the power of the Church. Religious and non-religious laws were separated. The latter came to be formulated on the basis of expediency and efficiency rather than ethics and religion, since it was believed that transformations in the general conditions no longer warranted their fusion. In Turkey, such a concept of the separation of State and Church did not come until 1924.

Instead, under Sultan Abdul Hamid, the empire continued to bask in a 'nomocracy,' shielded from constitutional and liberal ideas by a Sultan who suppressed the press and either executed or banished liberal reformers. During his reign, educational, judicial, and legal reforms were carried out. Improvements in the means of communication, in railways, roads, and telegraphs, were also fostered. He encouraged these changes, however, in the hope of strengthening the empire and maintaining his power over his subjects.

With this objective in mind, and mindful of the power of the Muslim religion in his domain, Abdul Hamid started taking greater advantage of his power as the twentieth century began to unfold. To counterbalance the impact of Western ideologies, of liberalism and constitutionalism, he turned to the tool of religion. He hoped to rejuvenate Islam's antagonism to the West and check its dangerous influence, thereby maintaining his own power. In support of the cause of Islam, he contributed half a million Turkish pounds for the Damascus-Hejaz railway to enable pilgrims to visit Mecca. This was a timely and powerful stroke, but it failed. By 1914, the religion had been weakened and almost eliminated as a weapon to be used for rallying the support of the whole empire in the defense of the Islamic faith. Political independence in the Arab provinces, inhabited largely by Muslims, was increasingly thought more important than religious unity in a crumbling empire.

B. *Social Structure*

Between the fall of Constantinople in 1453 and 1914, the population of the Ottoman Empire has been broadly classifiable into three distinct categories. The Muslims, particularly the descendants of the original Ottoman invaders, constituted the first category. Although they mixed with other races and lost their purity, they continued to dominate the management of the state; they manned the government, the army and the religious hierarchy. Ministers, governors, Ulema, and a host of subordinates comprised the bulk of this group.[4] The *rayahs,* primarily Greeks, Jews, Armenians and Franks, made up the second category, the entrepreneurial class which directed industry, commerce and banking.[5] The last category contained the masses of the population, largely peasants and artisans who toiled under the burdens of exploitation.[6]

Another classification which brings out salient points in each group is that which divides the empire into *millets* (autonomous entities subordinate to the Ottoman body politic); there were Muslim, Greek, Armenian and Jewish *millets.*

The religious and civil power of each *millet* was delegated to an ecclesiastical dignitary, who exercised these powers under the political and military supervision of the Ottoman state. In effect, these powers constituted special rights and privileges. For instance, each *millet* enjoyed the freedom to manage its communal affairs, using its own methods and facilities to practice its own religion and rear its own children. Under each religious head, ministers, ambassadors and a host of subordinates performed several functions; they raised taxes, registered births, deaths, marriages and wills, and litigated civil disputes among their members in their ecclesiastical courts. This was possible because, though Turkish subjects, they were immune from Turkish law, presumably from the Sheri'at.

> The Christian subjects of the Porte have been taught to look upon their ecclesiastical heads as their immediate rulers and protectors and their allegiance has been primarily to them, or to their Church, and their feeling of loyalty or patriotism has been to them rather than to the Sultan.[7]

Thus, according to Toynbee, the *millet* system.[8]

> . . . encouraged the perpetuation of a separate communal life which eventually developed into a longing for an independent national life and gave opportunity of foreign 'na-

tionalisms' to grow up in the midst of the Ottoman peoples.[9]

a. *The Muslim Umma (Millet)*

As has been pointed out, the Muslims constituted the majority of the population in the Ottoman Empire. Of the total residents of 35,350,000 in the mid 1850's, Michelsen gives the following estimates:

"Mohametans residing	in Europe	3,800,000
	in Asia	12,950,000
	in Africa	3,800,000
	Total	20,550,000"[10]

The Muslim community in the Empire was composed of Turks, Kurds, Arabs, and some Europeans. It is regarded by Toynbee as the highest ranking *millet* ("Though the name 'millet' does not appear to have been applied to it technically").[11] Basically, the principles upon which this organization was founded were the same as those in the other *millets*.

> It lived under the Sheri'eh or Islamic 'canon-law' which was interpreted by the muftis (juris-consuls) and administered by the Khadis (judges), the "Grand Mufti' or Sheikhu'l-Islam at Constantinople being the head of the Islamic community. To this Islamic millet belonged the free feudal landowners and the peasants on their fiefs (in regions where these 'cattle' happened to be Muslims and not Christians), and also the converted members of the Sultan's slave household (though in practice, if not in theory, the Sultan's slaves were above the Islamic law).[12]

As will be demonstrated later, under the Ottoman economy, the Muslim majority was settled mainly in the interior and engaged primarily in agriculture. It provided manpower for the Sultans to fight in their many wars. In time of peace, the soldier became farmer, only to be called again in times of emergency, leaving the farm in the care of his family.

Broadly speaking, the Muslim peasants presented a sad situation. They were immersed in fatalistic attitudes, beliefs and prejudices which were hard to change. Their living conditions were miserable. Wars took their toll amongst them. They were ravished by brigands and famished by bad weather conditions. Their productivity was low, since they used outmoded and worn-out tools of production. Besides, their tax burden was heavy and they were often impoverished by debt. In consequence, they had no incentive for change and generally had very little hope of improving their economic well-being through greater productivity. In terms of Rostow's stages of development, one could see this group as belonging to the pre-Newtonian traditional stage where agricultural production has a ceiling; in this case, the ceiling was very low. But the following is stated of the class of merchants residing in Constantinople:

> There are very few Mussulman merchants of any importance, and these are generally dependent on the services of native Greeks and Armenians for the conduct of their business. There are of course a certain number of Mussulman shopkeepers and retailers, mainly in the Stambul bazaar.[13]

b. *The Greek Millet*

> The Greeks are the most intelligent race in this region, and possess the greatest wealth and commercial power. They divide with the Armenians the commercial activities of the country.[14]

As descendants of the late Byzantine Empire that collapsed after the fall of Constantinople in 1453, the Greeks constituted one of the most restive elements within the Ottoman Empire. Their number, heritage, wealth, and knowledge of various arts and skills lent support to their aspirations. They never forgot that their ancestors had ruled the empire that became Ottoman. It is not surprising, then, that they were regarded in Ottoman circles with fear and suspicion. They were nonetheless tolerated by the Ottomans; consequently, they played an active role in the building of the empire.

> The Turks, being a race of soldiers, needed the Greeks and other Christians for the other functions of the empire which

could not be successfully filled by Turks, especially in the early days of the Ottoman Empire.[15]

In the nineteenth century, after the Greek War of Independence (1823-29), the Greek population, now reduced in number under Ottoman jurisdiction, was treated with even greater mistrust. But the suspicion and hatred were mutual.

One method of discussing the Greek minority is to follow the Porte's treatment, that is, to consider the Greeks as members of 'Millet-i'Rum.' Out of the six non-Muslim *millets,* the Greek Orthodox was the most important in the Ottoman Empire. About 1856, it numbered around 6,600,000. The next largest was the Gregorian Armenian, counting 2,400,000 members.[16]

> Where did the Greeks reside and what were their occupations?
>
> The racial Greeks in Turkey, irrespective of nationality, have settled mainly in the coast cities. In this respect they carried on the traditions of the ancient Greek colonies. They have been most intimately associated with Smyrna, with the islands off the Western Asia Minor coast, with Pontus, and with Constantinople. Greek investments in Turkey have been confined largely to commerce, shipping, banking and industrial enterprise. Greek capital utilized in Turkey has largely been in liquid form.[17]

Although it has been generally maintained that the Greeks preferred to engage in services and trade, there were a few exceptions. Fraser, in referring to the industrial development in Cilicia, discusses the feats of the Greeks in this endeavor.[18]

c. *The Armenian Millet*

The Armenian *millet* was under the tutelage of the Gregorian Patriarch who lived in Constantinople. Estimates on the number of its members are, as usual, scanty and unreliable. Michelsen, as was pointed out, includes the Armenians with the Greeks in his 1854 estimate, giving a grand total of 13,730,000. On the eve of World War I, the total population of the Armenians in the Ottoman Empire was given at 2½ million out of an estimated total of 22 million.[19]

The Armenians, like the Greek and Jewish minorities, were active in the economic life of the Ottoman Empire.

> . . . they have controlled nearly all the domestic commerce and two thirds of the import and export commerce. They have established very important houses in England, in Italy, in France, in the two Americas, in Egypt, and in all the ports of the Levant. It required dexterity and some education. The goldsmiths, silversmiths, jewelers, sculptors, and mechanics of Turkey have been for the most part Armenians.[20]

d. *The Jewish Millet*

Finally, the Jewish inhabitants, primarily descendants of those who migrated from Spain and Portugal in the late fifteenth and early sixteenth centuries, comprised a very small but active minority in the life of the Ottoman Empire. The Jewish *millet* was under the Grand Rabbi, the Hakam Effendi. Around 1854, the Jewish population was estimated at 170,000, 70,000 of which lived in the European section and the rest in Asia.[21] In 1914, an estimate stood at half a million.

Rather than settling inland, the Jewish inhabitants also took up residence in and near seaports

> . . . because the latter offer facilities for quick exit in troublesome times. In fact, nowhere in the Ottoman Empire have they settled at a distance of more than sixty to seventy kilometers from the shore. For example, there are settlements of Jews at Brusa (60 Kms from the port of Mudania) and at Magnesia (60 Kms from Smyrna.)[22]

Other reasons besides fear compelled them to live in ports. Since the Jewish population was particularly active in the commercial and financial aspects of the economy, and had neither the experience in or the desire to be engaged in agricultural pursuits, they resided in commercial towns and ports where their skill and knowledge could be put to fruitful use. The Jews helped in the establishment and operation of the Ottoman Bank and the Société Générale. They also engaged in other activities: for example, "The development of commerce in paper, hardware, colonial products, is due largely to the Jews."[23]

C. *Economic Consequences of the Social Structure or the Millet System*

On the basis on what has been discussed, the middle class in the Ottoman economy may be divided into two major groups: (i) the Effendis of Istanbul,[24] primarily made up of the administrative staff (the bureaucrats) of the ruling group and generally of the Islamic faith;[25] and the "rayahs" (an Arabic word meaning originally "cattle at pasture"). The latter were industrial, commercial and financial agents mostly engaged in the different aspects of production and exchange. In some instances, they also engaged, directly and indirectly, in the political activities of the state.[26]

Undoubtedly, the presence of the *millet* system created an unusual economic situation in the Ottoman Empire. As has been noted, in each one of the non-Muslim *millets*, there existed an entrepreneurial class primarily engaged in trade, both retail and wholesale; in financial business, especially banking; and in shipping, particularly coastal. This class division led to the strengthening of the *millet* and the creation of greater solidarity within it. Furthermore, the advantages realized were also kept for the improvement of the individual *millet* concerned.

The Muslim *millet*, on the other hand, suffered from the absence of the intelligent and dynamic entrepreneurial class which was responsible for building the economic empires of Western nations. In Great Britain and in the United States, individual initiative in business and trade promoted economic growth. With the full support of an advanced financial structure, the entrepreneurs in these countries were further helped by their respective governments and by the various social, economic, and political institutions. Non-Muslim entrepreneurs, as daring and as aggressive as the Britishers and Americans, were obstructed by a hostile social climate. Muslim entrepreneurs were few and wanting. Muslim Ottomans, with intelligence and education, had better opportunities and received greater assistance when seeking government employment than when embarking upon business activities.

The presence of minority groups engaged in entrepreneurial

activities has led many an observer to conclude that the Ottoman Empire in general lacked a middle class. This is true, of course, in absolute terms.[27] A summation of the activities, characteristics, etc., of the minorities should demonstrate, however, the relativity of this observation.

1. *Residence*: Except for the Armenians, many of whom shared central and eastern Asia Minor with the Kurds, the non-Muslim *millets* generally resided in and around seaports. It was remarked earlier that fear was a primary factor responsible for the choice of coastal areas for residence on the part of these minorities. But even during the Byzantine Empire, the Greeks had lived on the coast, where they conducted their economic activities, owned coastal shipping, and were possessed of a powerful fleet which afforded necessary protection. More recent sources discussing this same subject hold similar views with respect to the residence of minorities.

2. *Possessions*: Since they dealt principally in services, the minorities generally had to keep their assets in liquid form.[28] In addition to having businesses in the Ottoman Empire, they also had their own branches in Europe. Indeed, they invested in different European centers, not only in search of profit, but for reasons of security.[29] Their fears were not unfounded. Many incidents had happened prior to the Armenian massacres of 1894, 1896, and 1909, and subsequent loss of lives and assets prove this point. In some other instances, however, the minorities invested capital in land for purposes of speculation.

> Christian and Jewish usurers, further, took advantage of the Turk's need for money, of his long absences in military service, and of their consular protection, to wrest lands away from the peasants; often these lands were not cultivated by the usurers, but became mere objects of speculation, or bait to attract another indebted borrower.[30]

But further investments were marred by insecurity, the lack of a consistent and favorable policy on the part of the government, and at times, the demands for propitious concessions by potential investors which led to no investment at all.

3. *Limited Economic Motivation*: Motivated by parochial self-interest and bent on weakening the Ottoman Empire in the hope

of attaining self-rule, the non-Muslim *millets* devoted their energy to promoting their own welfare and living standard. They maintained a high level of education in the skills, the arts and the professions, but their knowledge was limited to the confines of each *millet*. Thus the businessminded middle class was detached from actual Ottoman life. Interested in attaining wealth and perpetuating its privileges, it was joined by a clique of foreign investors who also sought political and economic benefits.

Holding on to the secrets of know-how, the select few possessed a great technical advantage. A monopoly on the professions and skills eliminated future competition and assured continued high remunerations for their services and those of their successors. Therefore, large-scale diffusion of knowledge was prevented. Furthermore, the Ottoman Government acknowledged this situation and perpetuated it. Too enlightened a mass could create trouble for an autocratic regime.

4. *Reforms in the Millet System:* Serious attempts at reforms in the Ottoman Empire came late and had limited effect. The *Hatti-Sherif of Gulhane* and the *Hatti-Humayun* recognized the necessity for reorganizing the *millet* system. But it was not until later, in 1862 and 1863 respectively, that the Greek Orthodox and Armenian communities were placed under organic laws, which tended to decrease the power of the clergy and increase secular influences. A similar charter was granted to the Jewish *millet* in 1865. Unfortunately, reforms in the *millet* system were not fruitful. Their political gains overshadowed any possible economic gains. Instead of eradicating deep-rooted suspicions and producing harmony within the empire, the advent to the throne of Sultan Abdul Hamid in 1876 destroyed whatever gains had been won.

In brief, each *millet* organized itself into some form of guild to protect its own interests. It kept its knowledge of skills within its confines for fear that competition might drive out its members and their successors. On balance, it upheld the interests of the members of its *millet* as against the interests of other individuals within the state. Thus the creation and replacement of skilled personnel were kept low as years went by, and consequent remuneration high. Generally members of the non-Muslim *millets* established residence in coastal areas where they conducted their businesses. They refrained from embarking upon industrial development for the reasons expressed above. They were held back, not really by lack of initiative, but by a fear of pouring knowledge and funds into the development of an economy that might seek to destroy them. The revenue could be high, but so was the risk of loss. Finally, the lack of cohesion and good will within the Ottoman society contributed heavily to the destruction of the Ottoman Empire.

This would lead us to the obvious conclusion that the Ottoman Sultans of the nineteenth century and in particular, Abdul Hamid II, were not sincere in their intentions to carry out reforms. But even when they were, they lacked not only the technical knowledge required for reform, but also the proper means to implement it. Their grasp of the importance of industrialization for raising their national product and ultimately increasing their revenue and the standard of living of the masses was extremely limited. Even supposing that they did grasp the importance of industrialization, they still resisted its adoption. Any new ideas which demanded institutional changes in the social, economic or political structure were anathema to the ruling institution. The main concern of Sultan Abdul Hamid was to maintain the status quo without any major modifications and thus hold an autocratic grip on the empire. In addition, the dictatorial demands of power necessitated his recruitment of the educated and intelligent among the rising Muslim middle-class—the effendis—in order to run his political machinery, maintain security, man his army and navy, and defend his crumbling empire. The shift of human resources from public to private endeavors drained the economy of potential men who could have contributed to economic development, though it must be granted that many of these people had no other desire but to enter the government service.

Hence, in this triangular affair, the unwillingness to tackle the problem of progress goes a long way to explain why retardation persisted in the Ottoman economy. Without a concerted effort to create an assimilated community based on a sound foundation (in the miiltary as well as in all aspects of education—the professions, the crafts, the skills, languages and the establishment of research facilities for the advancement of acquired knowledge), that is to say, without the cooperation of an enlightened mass regardless of minority systems, little could be accomplished in the economic sphere.

With an almost totally rigid social structure,[31] with an illiterate and ignorant majority engaged in primitive agriculture, with the presence of an enlightened but wealthy minority bent on self-interest, and with a ruling body fraught with corruption and governed by tyranny, hope for any economic development was fruitless.

The situation might have been different had the Porte worked sooner on national unity and created a more cohesive and mobile structure. But such was not the case. In fact, how this empire existed for so long is cause for bewilderment. Emin frankly expresses his puzzlement when he admits,

> When one closely realizes the heterogeneity of the conditions they (the Turks) found in Asia Minor and Southeastern Europe, one cannot help asking: How was the whole thing possible? How could a great empire be built up on such a basis and maintained for more than six centuries? One becomes more and more puzzled by remembering that the founders of the Ottoman Empire were but a fraction of a single wandering Turkish tribe, and had to face, for many generations, a keen antagonism for all stocks kindred to them, religiously or racially, instead of support and help.[32]

CHAPTER III

THE OTTOMAN ECONOMY: 1856-1914

A. *Agriculture*

It has been pointed out that by and large, the majority of Ottoman citizens were Muslims engaged in agriculture. They are referred to as:

> . . . the simple children of the soil, they are the true conservatives: strict Muslims, following the traditions and customs of their ancestors in every aspect of life, and pursuing their agricultural profession along the same furrows that their ancestors drove a thousand years ago.[1]

Illiteracy, ignorance, conservatism in modes of thought, beliefs and attitudes, insecurity,[2] the tax system, lack of good means of communication, the incessant insurrections and wars which took their toll of manpower and resources: all of these conspired to weaken the economic position of the farmer and depress his condition. The situation of the farmer was a status quo which the government did little to improve.[3]

Even after World War I, the methods used in cultivation continued to be primitive,[4] though a few exceptions are noted.[5] Steam ploughs, reapers, very light metal ploughs were introduced, especially in the vilayets of Adana and Smyrna.

A look at the export-import figures of the Ottoman Empire[6] gives us an idea of the items produced locally and exported (excepting those items in transit), and those which were imported. Throughout the period under consideration, the tables consulted show a definite predominance in the export of agricultural products, particularly raw materials, and the import of manufactured goods.

On the export list, tobacco, grains and cotton take the lead, with mohair, sheep and lamb's wool, and valonia following.[7] Others of less importance include rice, honey, olive oil, fruits and vegetables, wine, opium, flax, hemp, silk, sugar cane, timber, resin, turpentine, cattle, gold, silver, iron, tin, lead, salt, marble, sponges and fish. Finally, with respect to imports from Great Britain, it is remarked that:

> The single most important manufactured article which held first place during the whole thirty years (1823-1853) was cotton cloth. After cotton, in order of importance, came refined sugar, iron and steel (exclusive of ore), woolens, i.e., yarn and manufactures, unwrought tin, and hardware cutlery.[8]

Before the promise of the *Hatti-Humayun* to establish a law which would allow foreigners to hold property in their name, no foreigner was permitted to own property in the Ottoman Empire.[9] The subsequent law of June, 1867, stipulated that foreigners could own property, except in the Hejaz, under the same conditions as Ottoman subjects. Though this new law removed an irksome barrier to foreign land ownership, there still remained the prohibition against foreign corporations holding real property in their own name. The law of 1913 indirectly allowed foreign investors within Turkish companies to own property in towns and villages, subject to the approval of the government.

For purposes of identification and taxation, landed property was divided into five classes: (i) Cultivable, called 'mulk,' was subdivided into several categories. (ii) 'Vakuf' or 'Mevkufe,' referred to land held by Muslim religious institutions. (iii) 'Mirie' or 'Erazi,' was land owned by the state. (iv) The land serving general use was named 'Metruke,' such as public roads, pasture grounds and places of prayer. (v) Finally, 'Mewat' was waste land, neither built upon nor cultivable, rocky hills, etc.

Concerning the Vakuf, some reforms were undertaken. Since the Ottoman Empire was in financial straits after the Crimean War, every attempt was made to increase the revenue of the state. One of these attempts included the Vakuf Reform of 1867.

> One small breach in the substance of Islamic law was made by Aali and Fuad in 1867, in the dangerous matter of *Vakuf*.

> *Vakuf* was the designation of property held in mortmain by various religious institutions such as mosques, dervishes, tekkes, and medressehs, wherein young devotees were trained in Moslem law and tradition. It was estimated that well over half of the property in the Ottoman Empire was held in *Vakuf* in the 1860's.[10]

The intent of this reform was to release much land for active cultivation, thus giving rise to increased yield from taxes on property and on produce.

B. *Mineral and Forest Resources and Fisheries*

The Ottoman Empire had been reputed to possess a large wealth of mineral resources, concentrated primarily in its extensive mountain ranges and in the Anatolian plateau. But even after World War I, no accurate or even a reasonable estimate of the potentialities of Turkish mineral resources was available. A few companies were finally allowed to investigate potentially wealthy regions and even invest in mining.

Leading in mining investments were the French. Their enterprises included:

> . . . the Heraclean coal mines near the Black Sea Coast, the Balia-Karaidin lead silver mines of Western Anatolia, the Ak Dagh zinc and silver mines of Angora, the large interests in Bulgar-Maden lead-silver in Southwestern Anatolia and the famous Arghana-Madden copper mines.[11]

An important British investment of six million gold francs went into Borax. The Borax Company Limited operated in Western Anatolia. Concessions of the Bender-Eregli coal went to the Belgians and Germans. Concessions in the chrome mines of Western Anatolia, largest in the world, were secured by the German Krupp Company.[12]

Mineral resources in which Turkey abounded include emery, chrome, meerschaum, pandermite (borax), salt, coal and copper.[13] These were of world importance. Of lesser importance were such items as manganese, antimony, zinc, mercury, nickel, silver and gold.[14] Oil proved to be abundant in Mesopotamia.

Resources of coal as well as those of iron were limited. These deficiencies are often presented as the major factor responsible for lack of industrialization, though DuVelay has much in praise of the excessive richness of Turkey in all kinds of mineral resources, including copper, manganese, chrome, silver, iron, marble, etc.[15]

Regarding forest resources, the Black Sea Coast, the slopes of the Taurus and anti-Taurus mountains and Western Anatolia were the chief regions which produced timber. Pine, oak, beech, fir, yoke elm, evergreen oak, rock rose, juniper, poplar, olive and chestnut, etc. were available in abundance.[16] Deforestation gradually took place, however, without any organized effort at reforestation. Timber had been used for both individual and public use. The armies used timber at will for fuel. Also, when railroads were constructed, large amounts of timber were needed and cut for beds. The process of exhaustion thus continued.

The fisheries of Turkey were important in the Bosphorus. The coast of the Mediterranean abounded in sponges, the Red Sea provided mother-of-pearl, and the Persian Gulf yielded pearls. These activities constituted a fairly large source of income to the Ottoman treasury, though much of it had to be turned in to the Public Debt Administration. Since the fishing methods were antiquated and no great progress was possible up to World War I, income from these sources remained nonetheless depressed.

C. *Industries*

The Ottoman Empire, then, had little in the form of industry in the mid-nineteenth century; nor had it developed conspicuously in that respect by 1914. The bulk of manufacturing was done within the household for use and not for sale. The establishments that produced items for outside markets were predominantly of two types: those making consumers' goods from the products of the farm and the forest, and those producing miiltary goods for the armed forces. Capital goods industries were virtually non-existent. As will be shown in later chapters, the economic and political conditions for more rapid industrialization were not yet developed and the main theme of the later chapters will be to indicate that the conditions under which the railroad construction took place in this era 1856-1914 were not such as to reduce sufficiently the major barriers of lack of capital, lack of technically trained labor, and lack of stable investment situation.

In Constantinople and the surrounding vicinity, a few flour mills, tanneries, rug and carpet works, cotton and woolen mills, tobacco depots and factories for making cigarettes, soap and glass factories were reported to be in operation on a relatively large scale (relative to household production). Very few factories were scattered elsewhere in the empire, however. For example, the Turkish Government owned cloth mills at Kara Mursal and at Ismidt. These were equipped with new machinery and manufactured the khaki woolen cloth required by the army. The woolen yarn spinning mill at Panderma and the weaving mill in Smyrna were owned and operated by private enterprise. However, with most of the industrial establishments, foreign capital and foreign management were imperative for their success. The tobacco monopoly was managed by the French. The glass factory on the Golden Horn was under British management. The textile factories in Cilicia were owned and run by Greeks. In Constantinople existed an American-British combine dealing in light skins and sheep guts, which dressed and pickled the pelts and shipped them to the United States.[17]

This represents the extent of large scale industrial development, for, (throughout the empire) many of the industrial products—including copper and brass utensils, pottery, shoes, saddlery and crude farming tools—were made in the household throughout the empire.[18]

There is, as has been noted, a close relationship between the locally produced Turkish raw materials such as cereals, hides, skins, tobacco, wheat, etc. and the type of industries constructed. However, there existed no canneries or food-preserving establishments to make use of the abundant fruits, vegetables, nuts and fish in which Turkey abounded. But this is no surprise, since these industries were also new to the industrial West.

D. *The Ottoman Budget*

So far, much of our discussion has centered around the agricultural, industrial and financial organization within the Ottoman Empire, but has hardly touched upon the role of the Ottoman Government. Insofar as government planning of incomes and expenditures is concerned, one would have expected the Porte to make advance yearly estimates, analyze carefully the contents of the budget, and take notice of any maladjustments. For, how could a government properly and scientifically remedy an economic problem if it had no adequate knowledge of its contents? Unfortunately, such was not the case.

The first Ottoman estimate of annual revenue was drawn up in 1863, for the fiscal year 1863-64. The estimate given by Blaisdell for this amount totaled beyond fifteen million pounds sterling. Five years later, the Ottoman Government estimated its income at nearly twenty million pounds sterling, parts of which were spent for payment on the mounting debt.[19]

Prior to 1863, some writers have presented interesting, though avowedly rough, estimates of Turkey's financial position. Michelsen, for example, gives an amazing account of Turkey's receipts and expenditures for 1852. Out of a total revenue of T.L. (Turkish Pounds):[20] 7,310,000, the largest portion of T.L. 2,200,000 is derived from the tithes; from land taxes: T.L. 2,000,000; indirect taxes: T.L. 1,500,000, totaling T.L. 5,700,000. With regards to expenditures which amounted to T.L. 7,314,000, about three millions went to the armed forces; T.L. 1,950,000 was spent on the functionaries; and T.L. 750,000 was earmarked for the civil list of the Sultan.[21]

Around 1900, the figures stood at: total revenue equal to 346,198,000 Francs and total expenditures amounting to 327,194,000 Francs.[22] These figures are almost double those of the 1850's. While the increased revenue mostly came from increased taxes on expanding agricultural production and from the improvements in the method of their administration and collection by the agents of the Public Debt Administration (organized 1881, See Section on Finances), a large portion of the expenditures was used to defray expenses incurred relative to the debt, such as interest and amortization, and also to pay on the principal of the internal and external debt. A large part again went to the armed services.[23]

For the year 1913-1914, the actual receipts are given at T.L. 29,201,865, while actual expenditures stand at T.L. 35,329,950. Thus a deficit of T.L. 6,128,085 is noted. It is essential to bear in mind that these figures apply exclusively to the operations of the Imperial Government; local receipts and expenditures by the vilayets, sanjaks, municipalities are excluded.

E. *Finances*

With the advent of the industrial age in the eighteenth century, Europe not only industrialized at a rapid pace, but also improved its financial machinery to meet the new demands of an advancing capitalistic society. Credit was organized to support economic as well as governmental activities in times of both peace and war. Large scale industrial development as known to the West, however, never set foot on Ottoman soil. Modern financial problems did not fail to occur.

From its early inception, the inconveniences of barter and inadequate supply of specie tended to handicap the expansion of local trade. Although the introduction of paper currency in 1830 at first facilitated the growth of trade, the chronic financial difficulties of the government led to continued increases in note issues. At first handwritten, the notes were later printed and numbered and when the number issued became known, their purchasing power depreciated.

In June of 1849, the Bank of Constantinople was created. Its foreign origin is indicated by the fact that Alleon, a Frenchman, and Baltazzi, an Italian banker, were named directors by the Sultan. It only took two years for this bank to accumulate a deficit of T.L. 35 millions and be liquidated.[24]

The Imperial Ottoman Bank was established in 1856, and reorganized in 1863: a fine occasion for the Sultan to obtain another loan in exchange for the new concession. This bank was also run by foreigners and with foreign capital. It was assisted by officials from the non-Muslim minorities. Additional foreign banks were established during the period under consideration, but it is worth mentioning that local banks had been in operation for some time before the establishment of larger foreign banks. They were privileged to provide loans to the Sultan. However, the amount loaned was insignificant, and most of the capital needed by the Sultan had to come from abroad. This was particularly true after the Crimean War.

Foreign banks established during this period were primarily commercial banks. The capital loaned out came largely from abroad rather than from local deposits and thus failed to furnish machinery for mobilizing the savings of the community. In addition, the loans from these banks usually served to facilitate the more liquid types of enterprises. They did not commonly invest in industrialization.

Early in the 19th century, the Ottoman Empire began to experience financial difficulties.[25] After his succession, Mahmud II (1808-1839) sought a loan from Great Britain. The Government of His Majesty King George III proposed to advance a loan of £1 million, provided the repayment be made in kind, in the form of wood, wheat and coffee to be delivered to the British fleet stationed in the Mediterranean. This loan did not materialize.[26]

A later attempt to provide a loan also fizzled.

> In 1838 Ponsonby (then British Ambassador at Constantinople) used his influence to establish closer relationship of Turkey and Britain by means of a loan of £3,000,000 which British capitalists were then negotiating. If the Sultan could be definitely obligated to Britain, British prestige might be raised, argued Ponsonby. Nothing came of this, however, because although the Foreign Secretary did not object to this transaction, he finally refused to guarantee the loan, and without this the English bankers refused to risk their money.[27]

The war in the Crimea, in which Turkey was allied with Great Britain against Russia and which started in 1853, triggered a new wave of spending on arms and armaments.

> During the Crimean War the Allies had lent money to Turkey and an inter-allied commission, of which Sir Edmond Hornby was the British member, had been appointed to see that the money was properly spent.[28]

Motivated primarily by military and then by political and economic motives, the first loan, then, was secured in 1854. The Egyptian tribute to the Porte was used as collateral. According to Blaisdell,

The earliest of Turkey's foreign loans were contracted with her allies, England and France, and were destined to meet extraordinary expenditures necessitated by the struggle with Russia during 1853-1856. Expedients which had been previously employed by the Government in moments of financial embarrassment were insufficient in this emergency. The sums needed for purchase of war material and for payment of troops were larger than the bankers in Constantinople, accustomed to granting short term advances to the Government were willing to lend. A long term loan was the alternative.[29]

The financial situation continued to deteriorate after the Crimean War. More and more debt was accumulated until a default occurred in 1875. Once the war was over, additional loans were made to replenish the treasury that the war had left empty.

The financial chaos that reigned before and after the empire's default has been subjected to lengthy studies. As to the amount of money contracted by the Porte, Correa writes that "no less than fifteen loans were contracted, amounting together to a nominal amount of Frs. 5,297,676,000.[30] Blaisdell estimated the debt at over one billion dollars.

Between the default of 1875 and the Decree of Moharrem in 1881, the financial situation in the Ottoman Empire worsened.[31] The bilateral agreement which this Decree in fact represented was reached on the 12th of Moharrem 1299, or 20 December 1881, negotiated between the Ottoman Government and representatives of foreign bondholders, and sanctioned by the Sultan's Irade. It was agreed that a permanent Council of Foreign Bondholders be formed out of Anglo-Dutch, French, German, Austro-Hungarian and Italian Groups. The primary function of this Council was the administration and collection of revenues from tobacco, salt, wines and spirits, commercial stamps, certain fisheries and the silk-tithe in certain provinces. The other function was to make payments to foreign bondholders who held securities prior to this decree. It was estimated that 3,000 revenue-collecting agents were in the employ of the Administration by the end of 1882. Additional functions were added later, some of which had to do with the railways, as will be considered in the following chapters.

Thanks to the presence of the Public Debt Administration, the financial situation in Turkey began to improve.

> In general, it may be said that Turkish finances were in reasonably satisfactory condition from 1881 until 1914. Revenues showed consistent gains; railways were opening up the country and increasing the taxpaying ability of many sections; the foreign administrative body known as the Ottoman Public Debt gradually imparted a strength to Ottoman credit that had not been previously known. Though deficits existed in the budget—deficits that efficiency and economy would have rendered unnecessary—they were not alarming, as the growing wealth of the Empire much more than counterbalanced them.[32]

Though most works on this subject applaud the laudable efforts of the Administration which helped improve the financial situation in the empire, others are not so favorable.

> The Council of the Ottoman Public Debt—an important and justly celebrated financial organization which, from 1881 down to the cataclysm of 1911-1923, had administered a portion of the Ottoman Public revenues with beneficial results, not only for the bondholders but for the Ottoman Treasury. . . . Thus harm done to the Ottoman Empire by its Western creditors between 1854 and 1881 had in large measure been atoned for by the constructive work of the Debt Council between 1881 and 1914; and, finally, the bonds had not only been scaled down and consolidated, but (after their rehabilitation) had largely changed hands in the ordinary operations of the stock-market.[33]

Blaisdell, on the other hand, attacks the Public Debt Administration on the grounds that it was associated with imperialist powers and followed policies which were often detrimental to the interests of the Ottoman people. While our object is not to evaluate these activities, it must be borne in mind that valuable services had been rendered by the Public Debt Administration.

In conclusion, borrowed funds continued to pour in almost exclusively from external sources, and their proceeds to be used for non-productive purposes, first to meet war charges, then to stabilize the economy, then to please the Sultan. As more and more debt was amassed, a larger and larger portion of the wealth of the country had to pass from Turkey to foreigners. The fact that about one-third of the receipts of the budget after the Decree of Moharrem was issued went to paying for the debt, another third went to finance the armed forces, and the remainder for personal expenses, particularly in the Department of the Harem, explain why there was nothing left for economic development.[34] Therefore, very little capital was channeled towards railway construction and hence an insignificant amount towards economic development.

F. *Capitulations and Tariffs*[35]

It may be wondered why Turkey had not sought, in view of her financial difficulties, to raise the tariffs and thereby increase her revenue. The reason was found in the longstanding system of capitulations which had marked the relations between Turkey and the Foreign Powers.

After the fall of Constantinople, Mohammed the Conqueror extended to foreign nationals certain judicial, economic, and commercial privileges and immunities they had previously enjoyed under the Byzantine Emperors. The common belief of the time was that the law was personal and followed a person wherever he went. The Venetians, Genoese and later, the French, British, Germans, and Americans took advantage of these privileges and exemptions. In 1535, treaty engagements between Turkey and Foreign Powers stipulated that privileges given to one power were to be extended to the others. The United States joined the ranks of other Foreign Powers in 1830 in order to enjoy the privileges of the capitulatory regime. Capitulations had already been issued to the French in 1535, and to the British in 1604.

Some of the privileges and immunities included in the capitulation system are as follows: Foreigners were rendered immune from all local jurisdiction; they were to be ruled and judged by their own courts.[36] They were exempt from all local taxes. Foreign banks and commercial houses were not subject to Turkish supervision. Foreign Powers established their own postoffices, etc. Under such a system of privileges, abuses were innumerable and inevitable.

The system of capitulations was abrogated by the Young Turks on September 8, 1914, and finally abolished, along with the *Millet* System, in the Peace Treaty of 1923, which was ratified in Great Britain on 15 April, 1924.

Supplementing the system of capitulations and often operating within its framework were the tariffs.[37]

> The Convention of Balta Liman, as this commercial treaty was called, written by Reschid Pasha and Lord Ponsonby, provided that all the old privileges and immunities be confirmed; that the monopolies be abolished; and that Britons be allowed to trade freely anywhere in the Turkish dominions; that British merchants would be subject to the same taxes in the internal trade; that the 3 per cent import duty be continued; and finally that the export tax be limited to 9 per cent 'ad valorem.' The treaty was to become operative March, 1839.[38]

The fact was that from time immemorial, since that of Suleiman the Magnificent, only a 3 per cent 'ad valorem' on imports and a small anchorage fee were charged.[39] An export duty of 12 per cent was levied on native products. Goods shipped across Turkey, and in some cases those shipped between Turkish ports, were subjected to a levy of 2½ per cent. Such transit trade had also to meet the whims and caprices of ruling pashas, which were considered by British exporters as restraints on trade.[40]

In the treaty of 1862 between the leading powers, including the United States, import duties were to continue at 8 per cent "ad valorem," but the export duties were to be reduced from 8 to 1 per cent at the rate of 1 per cent annually. Attempts by Turkey at raising import duties in 1875 and again in 1893 were unsuccessful, for no general agreement could be reached that was satisfactory to every one of the powers.

After many years of diplomatic wranglings and manoeuvres, Turkey was finally given the green light to raise her customs duties from 8 to 11 per cent 'ad valorem.' In return, large concessions were given. The effective date of this increase was July 12, 1907. From then on, up to 1914, the tariff rates remained unchanged, although a foreign expert had been commissioned to work on the tariff system and customs administration.[41]

BOOK II

RAILWAY DEVELOPMENT IN THE OTTOMAN EMPIRE AND ITS ECONOMIC CONSEQUENCES

CHAPTER I

NON-RAILWAY MEANS OF TRANSPORTATION

A. *Introduction*

It has been shown in Chapter I that the Ottoman Empire was endowed with excellent ports, indispensable to the sea-transport from and to its shores. But aside from the Bosphorus Straits,[1] which split Constantinople, linked the Sea of Marmara with the Black Sea, and afforded a water link between Turkey in Asia and Turkey in Europe, few navigable waterways were of any commercial value. Unfortunately scattered all over the empire, none of them linked the different sea ports with the interior of Asia Minor, which was the center of agricultural and mineral wealth in the empire. Not only was internal water transport absent, but the empire had no good roads. Due to the topography of the country, roads were difficult and expensive to construct. A few paved roads existed, the main one being one between Constantinople and Adrianople, used primarily by the armed forces.

> In fact roads "were commonly regarded as less a useful means of communication than as possible routes for invading armies, as an aid to Christian merchants, and as means of spying on the empire."[2]

Most of the rivers in the Ottoman Empire were short, swift, and unsuited to navigation and commerce.

> The rivers of Anatolia are of scant present importance, since they are for the most part navigable merely for a short distance from the coast, and cannot be relied upon due to the frequent torrents in the rainy season and to the dry summer weather. Their possibilities lie more in connection with irrigation and with hydroelectric power. The main streams are the Sakkaria (Sanjak of Izmid) and Kizil Irmak (vilayet of Trebizond) which flow into the Black Sea, and the Su Sigirly

> Chai which flows into the Sea of Marmara, and the Sihan and Jihun (vilayet of Adana) which enter into the Mediterranean.[3]

Aside from the above-mentioned waterways, there were a few navigable rivers in distant provinces, particularly the Nile river in Egypt and the Tigris and Euphrates rivers in Mesopotamia. Their being at a long distance from the capital of the Ottoman Empire, however, limited their usefulness.

The rivers in Cilicia were of little importance.

> Three rivers that once bore the classic names of Sarus, Cydnus, and Pyramus, rise in the Taurus, Anit-Taurus, and Amanus Mountains, and make short passages across the plain to the Sea. The importance of these rivers is not to be measured by their length, but by their volume, which represents the winter's snow from three great ranges and the summer rain of a wide catchment area.[4]

The lakes in Turkey, few in number, had no apparent geographical or strategic importance, as evidenced by the fact that no proper exploitable use was made of them.

> Lake Van in the remote interior is the largest. It has an expansion of 1,425 sq. miles with depths of 327.5 ft. in the southern portion, which falls to 81.9 ft. in the western part. The water is extremely salty and while the lake is navigable there is no regular service. Tuzgolu (salt lake)in the center of Anatolia is a large shallow salt lake . . . Lakes Igridir and Beysehir in Western Anatolia are important sources of supply for fresh fish, while the former also is an important link in the transportation of grain from the interior plains to Smyrna via the Aidin railway, also lake Sabanca between the Sea of Marmora and the Black Sea.[5]

Dependence on the beast of burden was therefore inevitable.[6]

Camels, mules, horses, and donkeys transported persons and commodities. Horses and mules had also to pull chariots and carriages. For reasons of security and sociability, caravans of hundreds of beasts traveled together, studding the narrow mountainous paths.[7] In spite of their number, they continued to be subject to raids by brigands and nomadic tribes. There were other hazards as well, such as the attacks of wild animals. Frequent stops had to be made on the road in order to give rest to the animals and their drivers, and often to fight off brigands. The slowness of the traffic, the hazards of the roads, and the type of carriers used for transportation compelled high rates of transportation. Thus, the nature of the goods transported had to be confined to those considered luxuries of the time, such as spices and silk, which could fetch high prices to cover their total costs. Raw material for exports and imported manufactured goods became prized objects for transportation in the early nineteenth century and continued to remain so throughout.

By the nineteenth century, the rulers of the vast empire had come to realize the importance of a good means of transportation for different reasons. Their inability to wage successful wars, quell insurrections in far-flung provinces, and even to maintain local security became associated with a poor means of communication. Besides, increased demand for Turkey's agricultural products impelled some action for better means of transportation. Since natural waterways were unavailable and the motor vehicle was not yet on the road, anything that had to do with steam-propelled boats or asphalted roads had to be shelved, though exceptions will be noted in Mesopotamia. News of railroads transportation had trickled into Constantinople, however, some aspects of which were later to become appealing. Of course, there were economic, social, political, strategic, and other benefits that could not be denied. But the reasoning that hit the soft spot of the Ottoman rulers was simple: armies, the pride and joy of the Ottoman Empire, trained on up-to-date western methods of warfare, could be transported swiftly to warring areas. The consequence of this logic was never in doubt: the outcome of the fight then would not have to be questioned. The Turkish soldier, known for his toughness, endurance and valor, could wring victories instead of defeats, and regain his lost pride rather than continue to be humiliated. Furthermore, the authority of the Sultan would become more centralized.

War after war emphasized the fact that Turkey was deficient

in transportation. The appalling delays in the arrival of military personnel, food, ammunition and medical supplies played a major role in changing the outcome of the fighting and finally in Turkey's defeat. Though the above conclusion seems apparent, it will be shown later that stressing railway development, while disregarding or minimizing the importance of fundamentals such as industrial development, education, research activities, and the political, economic and social organization and administration, could be ruinous. In other words, lopsided development in social overhead capital—for railways in this case—is futile and detrimental unless backed by the concomitant changes important for balanced growth.

Drawing on a historical analogy, it may be recalled that it was the same problem that plagued the Roman Empire: transportation. The answer was then provided at that time in the building of hard surface roads. But when the empire succumbed, the roads were neglected. In the case of the Ottoman Empire, the answer to this old problem was the construction of railway lines. But this proved to be only one answer to one problem and not an overall solution at all.[8]

Other improvements in the means of transportation were started by the British in Mesopotamia, who experimented with steam boats along the Tigris and Euphrates rivers, hoping to find a shorter route to India. When their attempts were unsuccessful and further experimentation given up, some members of the Lynch family capitalized on the situation. Basing their action on the Imperial Firman of December 29, 1834, which was supplemented by a 1846 vizirial letter issued by the Pasha of Bagdad[9] regarding navigation along the Euphrates and Tigris rivers by British steam boats, the Lynch Brothers organized a company for the purpose of commercial navigation. Banking on the Porte's support and vying with unsuccessful competition from Turkish steam services, virtual monopoly of navigation rights was assured.

As the Lynch firm went into operation, it charged the rates the traffic would bear, and its business efforts were extremely successful. A profitable traffic, both in goods and passengers, between Bagdad and the Persian Gulf was developed. With a keen and futuristic business interest in the area, the Lynch firm ploughed back its profits, developing the economic resources of the Near East. This occurred after the Crimean War.

> In order to feed the Tigris line, they (the Lynch Brothers) opened up roads into Persia, placed steamers on the Karun which were sometimes operated at a loss, built bridges, and developed caravan routes."[10]

Aside from local competition, which at no time was serious, the German Bagdad railway enterprise, however, brought in its wake a series of difficulties. Finally, in 1914, the Lynch Brothers and Lord Inchcape, a British magnate of vast wealth and influence with the British Government,[11] merged their interests.

CHAPTER II

Railway Development in the Ottoman Empire[1]

A. *Introduction*

At the beginning of 1860, the Turkish Government published a "Book of Specifications" (Cahier des Charges) in which it presented her views to those interested in getting concessions in the empire. Those rules and principles were based in part on an early concession granted to a British company in 1856 for the construction of a line between Smyrna and Aidin.

Since most of the railway construction and operation in the Ottoman Empire in the period under consideration was undertaken by foreign investors, with the aid of the Ottoman Government, it is only fitting that discussion be focused upon these investors. In view of the abundant material that is available on this subject, only a brief survey is here presented.[2]

The country of origin of the investor, or of the capital invested, can be used as a starting point. For instance, British investment in railways will be taken up first, since the first concession was granted to an Englishman. Then the French, German, and other investments will be discussed at some length. Although this method of arrangement has some drawbacks, it is convenient. It should be said that some ventures were, in fact, undertaken jointly by various foreign investors, using capital amassed in various European cities. Mention of these and other facts will not impair the use of the above classification, however.

B. *British Investment in Railways*:

The interest of the British in constructing railways in the Ottoman Empire dates back to the 1830's, when Captain Chesney explored the possibility of building a line of communication joining the Syrian coast with the Euphrates and finally ending on the Persian Gulf. This project was opposed by Mehemet Ali.

The first real attempt to construct a railway line was made, however, in autonomous Egypt, which was under the nominal suzerainty of the Sultan (since she continued to pay tribute to the Porte till 1881). In 1835, with the blessings of Mehemet Ali, Galloway Bey, an Englishman, laid out plans for building a railway line between Alexandria and the Suez by way of Cairo. In anticipation of British support, he placed large orders with British firms. To Egypt were shipped iron rails, wooden ties and other railway equipment, but the project did not materialize and heavy losses were incurred. Twenty years had to elapse before it was finally accomplished.

> By the middle of the nineteenth century the vogue of railway building was in full blast. The steam locomotive had caught the popular fancy. Railways were expected to inaugurate a new era of communication, as much more rapid than the steamboat as that had been superior to the canal barge and the stage coach. At this time when considerable distances were actually being bridged by railway lines in England, on the continent of Europe, and in India, the first tangible step was taken toward investigating the possibility of building a great trunk line from the English Channel or North Sea to Constantinople, from Scutari to Basrah, and from the Persian Gulf to India.[3]

However, the British company, later a Turkish Société Anonyme, which received the first concession on September 23, 1856, for the construction of a railway line in the Ottoman Empire, had no such grandiose schemes. It was simply interested in running a line between Smyrna and Aidin, 373 kilometres long, which it was believed would be financially rewarding.[4] It was intended to penetrate the fertile Büyük Menderes river valley, develop the region through which it passed, provide a fast and reliable system of transportation that would enhance trade development between Britain and the Porte, and bring about personal as well as national gain.

The cities which the railway line connected were of immense commercial value. Smyrna, situated on a deep gulf on the Mediterranean, was a natural outlet for the highly rich and productive Asia Minor. For centuries the most important trade had converged upon this principal port. Aidin, on the other hand, was located in Anatolia and offered heavy agricultural and commercial activity.

Construction of the Smyrna-Aidin line, a standard-gauge single track, was made without any kilometric guarantees from the Porte.[5] Generally, guarantees were given to various railway investors at a later date to assure them a fixed gross income every year. But for financial reasons, it was not until the middle of the 1860's that construction was begun and the line finally completed.[6] This line was eventually extended to Ergedir, a distance of 470 kilometres. A branch from the main line to Buzdur, some 13 kilometres long, was also under construction. In the same year, the old concession to the British company was consolidated and the franchise extended to 99 years. The new concession not only empowered the company to construct new lines of 320 kilometres, but also conferred upon her navigation rights on lakes Ergerdir and Beyshehir. The war prevented the materialization of this scheme, however.

On the eve of World War I, it was estimated that British capital invested in the Aidin railroad amounted to about $50 million, or a third of the money invested in Turkey by the British Public.

The second concession was granted in 1863 to another Englishman, Mr. Edward Price, who transferred it in the same year to a British company, The Smyrna-Kassaba (Cassaba) Company. The concession empowered the construction of a railway line extending from Smyrna to Kassaba, a distance of 93 kilometres.

A preliminary extension of 75 kilometres from Kassaba to Aleshehr (Alashehir) was allowed in 1872. In 1888, the construction of a branch from Magnesia to Soma was authorized. Five years later, the Turkish Government exercised its right of purchase to buy out the British company for a sum of 35,850,000 francs (£1,434,000, i.e., £1 ≈ 25 francs) and sell it to a Franco-Belgian syndicate which eventually became the Smyrna-Kassaba Railway Company (Chemin de fer Smyrna-Cassaba et Prolongement). The new company was authorized to extend the main line from Aleshehr to Afium Karahissar. In 1910, a concession was given for the construction of a branch line from Soma to Panderma, on the sea of Marmara. It was opened to traffic in 1912, and on the eve of the war, Smyrna-Kassaba Company operated a line 684 kilometres long. But only the eastern section from Aleshehr to Afium Karahissar was under a kilometric guarantee.

The British were also fortunate in obtaining another concession for a third line, to run between Varna and Roustchouk, a distance of 220 kilometres. After its opening on the 17th of November, 1866, this line remained in the hands of a British company until purchased by the Bulgarian Government in 1886.

The Mersina, Tarsus and Adana Railway Company, also owned a line, 67 kilometres in length, which traversed the rich plain of Cilicia to reach the port of Mersina. The first concession was granted to two Turks in 1883. Then a Turkish company was formed in 1885 with Anglo-French control. Finally, in 1896, French and British stockholders bought the whole interests in the line, which was run without any guarantees, but had to sell it in 1906 to the Deutsche bank, whose officers had successfully frustrated the efforts of the company to secure extensions. In fact, the Bank needed an outlet to the sea for the Bagdad line, an outlet which was provided by the Mersina, Tarsus and Adana line.

Of minor importance was the Haifa Railway Company, a British company, which had received a concession in 1890 after it had started. The Haifa-Acre line, which was consequently opened in 1906, became a branch of the Hejaz railway.

Finally, it may be mentioned that the final section of the Bagdad line, from Bagdad to Samarra, was awarded to the British, just on the eve of the war in 1914.

C. *French and Austrian Investment in Railways*

French and Austrian capital was largely invested in the Balkan Peninsula where the British had constructed the Varna-Roustchouk line in 1866. A concession for the construction of the Rumelie line was first given to M.M.C. et L. Van Elots Fréres and Company. As it failed to raise the necessary funds, it relinquished its rights.

In 1869, an accord was reached between Baron Hirsch, a German, and the Porte. The former received a concession for building a network of 2,500 kilometres, extending from the

Black Sea to the Austrian border and joining the Danube with the Aegean Sea.[7] Most important of all, the contemplated line was to link Constantinople with Belgrade, which was already joined by a railway to Paris. In view of the obstacles facing the Austro-French company, a new arrangement had to be reached in 1872, whereby the length of the network was reduced and kilometric guarantees were secured.[8] By 1878, lines of about 1145 kilometres had been constructed. From Constantinople to Adrianople to Bellova, the distance covered amounted to 562 kilometres, from Dedeagatch to Kouleli to Bourgas: 114 kilometres, from Tirnova to Yamboli: 106 kilometres, and from Salonica to Mitrowitza: 363 kilometres.

After the Treaty of Berlin, a conference between Turkey, Bulgaria, Serbia and Austria-Hungary resulted in the Convention of May, 1883, in which each Government agreed to finish the remaining uncompleted line in its own territory before October 15, 1886. The Turkish Government was given charge of the Bellova-Vakarel, Vakarel being a terminal point on the Oriental Rumelie Frontier at a distance of 46 kilometres from Bellova. In addition, she found herself in charge of a line from Uskub to Zibeftche, which reached the Serbian frontier. The length of this line was estimated at 85 kilometres, thus making a total of 131 kilometres. The concession was ceded to Baron Hirsch, whose company began working in 1885 and finally completed it in 1888. The Uskub-Salonica railway was opened to Belgrade, and the Constantinople to Bellova line put the final touch on the network, thus reaching Bulgaria and Serbia. By 1888, a line of 1,686 kilometres linking Constantinople with Vienna was in operation.[9]

Surprisingly enough, the Baron finally ceded all the lines included in his concession, those both finished and unfinished, to the Deutsche Bank.[10] This was accomplished on April 17, 1890. But on the first of October of the same year, the Zurich Bank for Oriental Railways, established with 63 million francs from capital shared by German, Austrian and Swiss Banks, repurchased all these lines for 72,355,000 frs. However, until 1913, one of these, the Deutsche Bank, remained in virtual control of the Oriental Railway Company.

In the interim period between the purchase and repurchase, the Deutsche Bank was given a concession to construct and operate a line between Salonika (Saloniki) and Monastir, 219 kilometres (136 miles) long. It was transferred to the Anatolian Company, which operated it till the Balkan Wars. This line carried a guarantee of £572 per mile.[12]

In the meantime, another French group, including the Banque Imperiale Ottomane, secured a concession for a line running eastward 550 kilometres on the coast and joining the Oriental Railways near Adrianople. The Saloniki-Constantinople Junction Railway was constructed and operated by a French company with a guarantee of 15,500 francs on the gross annual receipts per kilometre.[13]

The Mudania-Brusa line, running from Brusa, the ancient capital of the Turkish Empire to its port Mudania, on the Sea of Marmara, has a unique history. Work on this line was started by the Turkish Government in 1873 and was interrupted later, due to financial and technical difficulties. However, a concession was granted to a Franco-Belgian company in 1891, good for 99 years. The distance traversed was 41 kilometres. The rail constructed was of a narrow gauge and the line carried no kilometric guarantees.

The largest and most distinct investments in railways, however, were in Syria (Syria, Lebanon and Palestine); these began to take shape towards the end of the nineteenth century. A special but small concession went to an Ottoman subject. In turn, he ceded it to a French company formed in 1889. This company constructed the line between Jaffa and Jerusalem, a distance of 87 kilometres, and added branch lines to Ghazza, a distance of 75 kilometres, and to Nablus, 50 kilometres. The work was completed in 1892.

Another concession was granted to a Lebanese, who ceded his rights to a French company which eventually constructed and operated the line between Damascus, Homs, Aleppo and Biredjek. The French company later became Société Ottomane du Chemin de Fer Damas, Hama et Prolongement or D.H.P. for short. It constructed the exceptionally narrow-gauge line of 1.05 metres between Damascus and Mäzarib in the Hauran, 97 kilometres long. It was opened in 1894.[14]

Fr. Company

The same company took charge of constructing the Damascus-Beirut line without any kilometric guarantees, the distance covered being 145 kilometres. It was in operation in 1895. Again, in 1902, a standard gauge line was opened between Riyaq, a town in the Beqa', which is located on the Beirut-Damascus narrow gauge, and Hama, 182 kilometres away. Four years later, the line was extended to Aleppo, another 137 kilometres. In 1909, a 97 kilometres standard gauge extension was constructed between the port of Tripoli and Homs, located on the Riyaq-Aleppo line.

On the eve of the war, the D.H.P. was in charge of running a 644 kilometres network of railroad, connecting the principal cities of Syria with the coastal periphery.

Other French promoters were awarded a railroad concession in 1908 to connect the Red Sea port of Holeida with Sana'a. This had for its purpose the diversion to trade from Aden into Turkish territory. The line was never constructed.

Final but significant concessions were given to French promoters as late as April, 1914. These were mostly for a network to be run in Northern Anatolia and Armenia. The grants were conditional upon badly needed French financial assistance.[15]

Just to get a bird's eye view of British, French and German investment in railways, in Turkey in Asia, Earle maintains that

> . . . until the Bagdad Railway concession was granted French financiers held the lead in the number of kilometres of railway in operation or contracted for. The situation in 1898 was as follows:

British	*Kilometres*	*French*	*Kilometres*
Smyrna-Aidin	373	Smyrna-Cassaba	512
Mersina-Adana	67	Jaffa-Jerusalem	87
		Beirut-Damascus	247
Total	440	Damascus-Aleppo	420
			1,266

German	*Kilometres*
Haidar-Pasha-Ismid	91
Ismid-Angora	485
Eski-Shehr-Konia	444
	1,020

All the British and German lines were in operation in 1898, whereas the French Syrian Railways were only partially completed.[16]

By 1914, French investment in railroads exceeded half a billion francs, and this was only a part of the large investment made by the French.

> The French holdings of Turkish public debt and investment in Turkish enterprises exceeded that of any other country. Of the twenty-six loan emissions of the Turkish Government between 1854 and 1914, French investment in railroads exceeded half a billion francs; vast further concessions secured in 1913-14 provided for 2,300 kilometres of new construction and still larger investment. French capital controlled the Banque Imperiale Ottomane which with its sixty-two branches, was Treasurer-General and fiscal agent for Turkey.[17]

D. *German Investment*

The Ottoman government's desire to link with the various provincial capitals led to the decree in 1871 of the construction of an Anatolian railway line, starting in Constantinople. "The following year a German engineer, Wilhelm von Pressel, drew up a ten-year master plan for a line extending from the Bosporus to the Persian Gulf, a distance of 2,700 kms. Thirty years later this plan was elaborated and modified."(1)

In the final months of 1888, a German Syndicate, later to become the Anatolian Railway Company (The Société du Chemin de Fer Ottoman d'Anatolie) and financed by the Deutsche Bank of Berlin, took over from Turkey the Haidar-Pasha-Ismid line of 90 kilometres.[18] This line had been constructed by the Turkish Government in 1871 and leased for twenty years to a British company in 1880. However, under German influence, the Porte took advantage of a clause in the contract to break the lease and permit the Germans to take over. This constituted the start of a larger design. Eventually, an Imperial Irade was secured in

---

(i) Issawi, Charles, editor, The Economic History of the Middle East 1800-1914. p. 91. The University of Chicago Press, Chicago & London 1966.

order to extend the line to Angora (Ankara) for 485 kilometres. The total distance from Haidar Pasha to Angora was placed at 575 kilometres.

In order to run the line, the company was granted a kilometric guarantee of 15,000 francs per kilometre. An additional guarantee of 10,300 francs per kilometre for the section between Haidar Pasha and Izmid was also provided. The concession was to last for 99 years after the line was opened to traffic, which took place in 1892.[19]

Then, to have the important line constructed between Eski-Shehr and Konia, a distance of 444 kilometres, the Porte offered the Germans a concession, embodied in the Imperial Irade of February 15, 1893. It carried an annual kilometric guarantee of 15,000 francs per kilometre. Payments were to be made under the supervision of the Office of the Public Debt Administration. Three years later, in 1896, it was completed and opened to traffic. This line, considered a branch line at the time, was regarded as of primary importance for the Bagdad line, to be built later. Besides, it was held in especial esteem since it passed through Afium Karahissar, thus establishing a connection between Smyrna and Constantinople.

The one line the Germans were highly concerned about constructing and operating was the Bagdad railway.[20] Many ambitious economic and political expectations depended upon the completion of this line. In the meantime though the influence of the Foreign Powers came to bear upon the Porte, Abdul Hamid was more susceptible and acquiescent to Germany than to the rest. The outcome was resolved in the signing of a preliminary Convention between Dr. Siemens, then Director of the Deutsche Bank, and the Porte in 1899.[21] The formal Convention was approved by the Sultan three years later. On March 5, 1903, the final agreement was signed. On the same day, the Imperial Ottoman Bagdad Railway Company was formed, with a capital of £600,000.[22] By 1914, the capital of the company controlled by the Deutsche Bank and its groups amounted to £5,400,000.[23]

The concession of the Bagdad railway carried with it handsome and liberal terms. The guarantees for the construction of the line were rewarding. In brief, they amounted to 15,500 francs a year per kilometre. This amount was to be capitalized with the Porte, giving the company State bonds bearing interest at 4 per cent, redeemable during the period of the concession. Besides, the Turkish Government undertook to provide a sinking fund at the rate of 0.0875 per cent. The remainder, 4,500 francs per kilometre, were allowed for working expenses. Once the line went into operation, if gross kilometric receipts exceeded the estimated remuneration over costs, a formula was worked out whereby the surplus was shared between the parties involved.[24] Besides, the revenues of the districts traversed were to be set aside for debt service, and put under the supervision of the Public Debt Administration.

> The 'Bagdad bahn' was destined never to be completed as planned by German interests. Begun soon after the original act of concession of March 5, 1903, it languished after the first section was completed the following year because of obstacles of all kinds—physical, financial, and political. Originally intended to extend from Scutari, opposite Constantinople, to the Persian Gulf, it had eventually to find a terminus in Bagdad.[25]

The first section of the Bagdad line, extending from Konia to Bulgurlu, a distance of 200 kilometres, was not difficult to construct since it traversed a flat region. But when further extension of this line was up for discussion, more than physical obstacles were hurled in its way. The rival Powers of Germany finally became aware of the danger to their interests in the Ottoman Empire.[26] But agreement for the second and third series of the Bagdad Loan Contract did not come until 1908, hardly two months after the re-establishment of the Ottoman Constitution in June, 1908. It was signed by the two parties concerned: the Porte and the German company. No time was wasted in having the second and third series of the Bagdad Railway bonds underwritten by the same syndicate which had taken the first series. Among the minor modifications introduced in the new contract was the extension of the Bagdad line from Bulgurlu to reach El Helif, a distance of 850 kilometres instead of 800, as was originally agreed.

After so many delays and obstacles, the second section was finally begun in 1910. Its building was particularly costly since parts of it had to go through mountainous terrain.[27] Finally, a new Convention was signed between the Bagdad company and the Turkish Government, in which the former was obligated to proceed with the third section from El Helif to Bagdad, 600 kilometres long.[28]

While a large part of the Bagdad line was built by World War I, the Taurus tunnels were not pierced until November, 1916. Only then was the traffic opened between Constantinople and Bagdad.[29]

Of minor importance is the Metropolitan Railway of Constantinople, which operated a line from Galata to Pera, a very short underground cable. In 1911, its concession was transferred from British hands to the control of the Deutsche Orient.[30]

Finally,

> German investment in industrial ventures in Turkey grew from virtually nothing in 1880 to independent importance before the war—from about 40 million marks to over 600 million marks. This investment was concentrated mainly in the Bagdad Railway of which about 2,000 kilometres had been constructed by 1914.[31]

E. *Concessions to Italians, Russians, and Americans*

Neither Italy, nor Tzarist Russia, nor the United States had owned or operated any railways in the Ottoman Empire. Italy had provided labor in some instances to help out in railway construction. She also laid claim to franchises in Southern Asia Minor: to a line from Aidin to Makri, and to another from Ergedir to Mersina. Such franchises never fructified.[32]

Around 1900, Tzarist Russia, already engaged in railway construction in its own territory, sought concessions to construct railways in the Ottoman vilayets bordering upon the Black Sea. The purpose behind the acquisition of these rights and privileges was to block German intentions of constructing railways in those areas. Since neither the German nor Russian investments ever took form, the French were able to take advantage of the world situation and the pressing financial needs of the Porte to acquire, just before World War I, a new concessions for a railway system stretching from Eregli to Van. These grandiose plans were never applied.

Similarly, an American group, headed by Rear Admiral C. M. Chester, initialed negotiations for railway concessions in 1908. These negotiations lasted till 1911. European, especially German and Russian influence, came to bear unfavorably on the Porte. On the other side, the American group began facing difficulties in trying to raise capital for the proposed venture. In consequence, these negotiations were also suspended.[33]

D. *Turkish Lines*

In the early days of railway investment, the Turkish Government undertook to construct the line of Mudania-Brusa. Work on this line was started in 1873, under Sultan Abdul Aziz, but due to financial and technical difficulties it was discontinued. In 1891, a 99-year concession without any guarantees was awarded to a Franco-Belgian group.[34]

The only line in the Porte's possession was the narrow-gauge railway known as the Hejaz line. Starting from Damascus, it traveled 1320 kilometres to Mecca. Though it was opened in 1908, it was not completed until 1914.

Ostensibly, this line was built for religious reasons. All collections were in the form of contributions and donations. Even the construction of the line was carried on by the Turks, with the help of foreign engineers.

> In the belief of many, the line was built for strategical reasons to enforce Turkish sovereignty among the Arabs, who have always been loath to admit the Sultan's claims to the caliphate.[35]

F. *Conclusion*

In conclusion, the lack of natural waterways and good roads in the Ottoman Empire necessitated the construction of railways which had immeasurable benefits to the Ottoman and world economies. Also, these railroads were built, financed, and operated by foreign companies, so that, by the end of the 19th century, Turkey had 4500 kilometres of railway lines: 1993 in European Turkey, and the remaining 2507 kilometres in Asiatic

Turkey. On the eve of the war, Turkey had about 5,252 kilometres of railroad. Its nominal invested capital was estimated at about 45 million Turkish pounds.[36] Further illumination on the subject of railroad investment and the extent of railroad construction is provided in the aforementioned series of tables in the appendix.

Historically, the development of railways falls into two major categories. In the first category are grouped the short lines that linked the interior with the sea-ports, such as the Smyrna-Aidin line. These lines preceded those in the second group, which principally connected different cities in the interior. The Bagdad railway falls in the second category.

As had been pointed out, a large area, about half the country, remained untapped by railways. While war brought to a halt major construction works, over a decade had to pass before any additional planning and construction could be undertaken under Kemal Ataturk. Nonetheless, for a country that had suffered from the absence of a good means of transportation, the arrival of railroads must have been a boon. To the impact of these railroads upon the Ottoman and world economies we now turn our attention.

CHAPTER III

PART I

Economic and Non-Economic Gains to the Ottoman Empire and to Foreign Investors and Powers

A. *Introduction*

The simplicity of exposition adopted in the previous chapter in its description of railway development in the Ottoman Empire between 1856 and 1914 was not intended to obscure the confused and intricate background that underlay this development. Political intrigues, the use of threats, bribery, favoritisms, and false promises of all kinds filled this background.[1] The previously described conditions in the empire favored the interplay of these forces, both from within and without. The rapidity of the rise and fall of ministers in the Ottoman Government gave a colorful but inconsistent policy to the Porte. Neither proper guidance nor direction seemed possible. On the other side of the fence, Foreign Powers entered into keen rivalries to curry favor with the Porte, wrench concessions from it, and enjoy its economic as well as other privileges.

Regardless of this hectic background, a partial railway network had been constructed. But, as has been remarked, most of the railway lines, with the exception of the Hejaz line, were owned and oprated by foreign investors using foreign capital. The Germans, though latecomers to railway development of the empire, held a large share on the eve of World War I; so did British and French investors.

The railway lines had been built over half a century, yet, considering the area of the empire, they remained mostly short and scattered in various provinces. The north and northeastern parts of the empire had no railways at all. It must be stressed that in the absence of a central coordinating authority to plan and guide railway development, an overall pattern was impossible.

However, a comprehensive plan for railway construction in Turkey in Asia, had been drawn up by the German enginner Von Pressel as early as 1872. The Bagdad line was a part of this scheme. Rivalries among the Foreign Powers subsequently necessitated various modifications in this and in other plans. No comprehensive scheme for railway construction could have passed the barriers of financial difficulties, international competition and rivalries, or the wavering policies of the Porte. Again, perhaps in view of the confused state of affairs—economic, financial, political, military, social and administrative conditions in chaos—requesting an overall was asking too much. Railway construction and operation fell instead into spheres of influence, where short lines were constructed at a time, serving a variety of purposes with varying degrees of priority. Investors in these spheres of influence sought to serve their own interest by trying to enlarge their concessions and to make the best use of them. In doing so, they were only conforming to the general pattern of rational entrepreneurship. However, when governments influence the investors, or else share in the investment process, political as well as the economic interests become crucial. In this vein, much has been said about the economic and political penetration of Germany into the Ottoman Empire.[2]

B. *Expansion of Trade Facilities*:

It was noted earlier that caravan transportation was slow (about three miles an hour), expensive, inflexible, and ineffective in moving bulky commodities, especially for long distances. Hence very small storage sheds were required and extensive improvements in docks and harbors were not needed. But with the advent of railways, many of which were built on established routes and connected already existing centres,[3] changes and improvements were deemed essential in these centres. The new system of transportation made feasible the expansion of traffic and the hauling of particularly large commodities.

> The railways carry to the seacoast principally bulk products, such as wheat, barley, wool, mohair, tobacco, and dried fruits. The quantity of minerals transported is almost negligible. There are practically no industrial establishments of any kind in the interior, so this important class of goods does not figure among the freight items. Railway

rates are high and ship rates so low in comparison that there is only a small amount of merchandise that can stand long rail carriage; moreover, as already stated, sea routes are preferred. Since the imports from abroad are largely consumed by the more prosperous residents of the sea coast cities, the amount of traffic on the railroads destined for the interior is much less than that in reverse direction, a situation true of animal transportation as well.[4]

Therefore, railroads gave impetus to the expansion of agricultural production, for which a demand was increasing in the industrial centres of the West. It also led to assigning greater importance to certain ports, a fact which later called for some adjustment by the Ottoman Government. One of these was Smyrna, which consequently became a much more important trading centre than Constantinople. The Porte took note of this and began to attach greater importance to Constantinople, making it the terminal or the main junction of the important railway lines going into the interior. But Constantinople still failed to attract more traffic than Smyrna. Commenting on the importance of the latter, Fraser writes:

> Smyrna is the ancient outlet for the trade of Asia Minor, and most of the important caravan routes converge upon it. The tendency for commerce to gravitate towards the markets of the world along the lines of least resistance remains true whether transport is by railway or cart or camel. No sooner was the Smyrna line linked up with the Anatolian system than exports from the central plateau of Asia Minor began to show an inclination to desert the Constantinople route and to revert to the old one to Smyrna. For instance, grain from Konia could be passed along the Anatolian line to Afium-Kara-Hissar, transferred there to the Kassaba line, railed to Smyrna and shipped more cheaply than if it were sent through Constantinople. The consequence was a raising of rates between Konia and Afium-Kara-Hissar which defeated this tendency.[5]

Then, as railway lines were constructed, railway stations had to be built and personnel engaged to run them, that is, to sell tickets; load, unload, repair and maintain lines and locomotives; and perform other minor functions. In addition, accommodations for the employees, travelers, and for goods transported had to be provided. Large storage houses were important and had to be furnished. In Smyrna, for example, the Aidin Railway Company built extensive warehouses, sheds and a large pier for steamers. In Constantinople, Beirut, and in other ports, extensive port improvements were carried out and were still being planned.[6] In every aspect of improvement and construction, income was generated. Undoubtedly, the purchasing power of the recipients and their standard of living were improved and enhanced. But because the Ottoman Empire was relatively underdeveloped and poor, much of this income was channeled into purchasing consumers' goods.

While in some instances, the construction of additional facilities was necessary in already established towns, in other cases new towns emerged, though these were the exception rather than the rule.[7] Where previously were small villages of no significance, now emerged prominent railway centres.

The following account is given of the rise of Eski-Shehr (Eskishehir), where development was remarkable after the railway construction in 1892.

> A mere village in pre-railway days, German enterprise has changed it into a flourishing town. Being selected as the principal depot of the railway, it quickly sprang into prominence, and it is one of the busiest places in Anatolia. The railway alone represents a population of 60 families, the adults of whom are drivers or guards for the trains, engineers for the workshops, or porters to deal with the heavy traffic. The total rolling stock of the system, said to number 50 locomotives and 2,000 carriages and trucks, is housed and repaired at Eski-Shehr. The workshops are largely and finely equipped, all the plant, said to be worth several hundred thousands sterling, coming from Germany.[8]

Again, with reference to Cilicia,

> Thirty years ago Cilicia had no dealings with the outside world, nor with parts of Turkey other than those im-

> mediately adjacent. Today there is a great production of cotton, a large proportion of it ginned, spun, woven on the spot. Seventy thousand bales is the annual product, part of which is exported to Europe raw, the remainder is in a manufactured condition being dispatched inland, wherever, and as far as, transport facilities offer.[9]

Needless to say, the extension of railways and the rise of new railway centres like Eski-Shehr gave an impetus to population movement into those areas, some of which was in fact forced by the Government. Konia is a case in point.

> Konia is the scene of an endeavour on the part of the Turkish Government to populate a wide region that only needs inhabitants to blossom forth into great productivity. Even the Sultan cannot augment the population, either by natural or supernatural means, so that the civilized device of immigration has been employed. The Government keeps agents in the Crimea, the Caucasus, Roumelia, and elsewhere to invite Mahomedans to transfer their place of residence.[10]

Fraser further adds:

> The Konia plain is peculiarly adapted for the production of cereals, and where very little grew before the arrival of the railway, there is now a largest harvest which finds a market at the coast. The railway has done so much for Konia undoubtedly, but not unaided. Konia and the neighborhood has been the scene of a considerable immigration experiment which has cost the Government a lot of money, and conferred no great gain on the immigrants, for the bulk of them would give their cars to return to the country whence they came. . . . There has further been a considerable gravitation of Anatolian peasantry to the railway country, a process that merely enriches one district at the expense of others.[11]

The development of railway centres undoubtedly gave new life to the surrounding community. Land values went up, giving rise to speculation. Lands previously left idle were cultivated and the surplus products shipped for export. Incomes were generated and small shops, hotels, restaurants, etc. became the nucleus of the towns.

C. *Development of Agricultural Resources*

Thus, above everything else, the arrival of railways provided an incentive for expanding agricultural activities. When matched with an increasing foreign demand, such expansion was not only inevitable but attained wide dimensions. Similarly, increased activities in the commercial and financial spheres followed suit. With railways traversing fertile areas such as the Anatolian region and the Cilician plain, regional as well as national development in agriculture could no longer wait.[12] Farmers, earlier content with producing small quantities for local consumption, embarked upon a more intensive program of production, the products of which they could market in distant lands.

> In former times the peasant cultivated enough for his needs and no more. It may be true that he is naturally indolent, but a more important cause of his want of enterprise was the impossibility of disposing of his surplus produce. In the districts traversed by the railway, this obstacle has been removed, and of later years the Anatolian peasant has shown that he is quick to learn and ready to use his opportunities. The railway has also mitigated the danger of famine, formerly very serious, as it is now possible for the products of a prosperous region to be sent to parts where the harvest has failed.[13]

With markets capable of absorbing the surplus, the Turkish farmer doubled his efforts. Furthermore,

> Every branch of export trade of Constantinople was expanding during the last few years before the war. The trade in cereals was growing with remarkable rapidity owing to the Anatolian Railway. The railway was also bringing to Constantinople new and important classes of goods for export. Of these, eggs and skins deserve a special mention.[14]

Even with the continued use of old methods and techniques of production, the presence of large tracts of arable land thus rendered possible a larger amount of production than before.

In order to market the agricultural surplus, it was necessary for the entrepreneur to expand his role as an intermediary between the farming community and the Western World. Assisted by the presence of active Ottoman minorities in the coastal regions and supported by foreign entrepreneurs and capital, banking, shipping, insurance, travel and other types of institutions were established. Some of those already in existence were expanded to cope with the new situation.[15]

The question then arises, how is one to measure and evaluate the extent of agricultural development resulting from the railway transportation system? If it were possible to isolate the impact of railroads from other factors, the answer to this question would not be as difficult as it presently looms.

D. *Indicators for Agricultural Expansion*

1. *The Land Indicator*

Perhaps the easiest way to find out how railroads affected agricultural production would be to obtain comprehensive statistical data on land cultivated before the railroad age and compare them with those that followed railroad development. Though a partial picture may be attained, such a solution is not feasible, due to the non-availability of accurate statistical data. Besides, it is extremely difficult, if not impossible, to isolate the impact of railroads from other factors such as population changes, reforms, changes in foreign demand for Turkish goods, changes in national income due to developments other than railroads, and martial activities. Besides, these and other factors—for instance, governmental policies—interacted with railway development and may be considered results as well as causes of development. Undoubtedly, certain areas may be isolated and distinctly shown to have developed primarily as a direct consequence of railways. But, on the whole, this process is not adequate.

It is worthy of note that Turkish farmers did not automatically acquire new lands and pursue plans for large cultivation. There were instances where their initiative prevailed, making possible an increased agricultural production. But outside assistance was essential and could not be discounted. Some irrigation schemes had been contemplated by foreign companies mainly associated with railroads, and with multifold purposes as well:[16] these were mainly connected with the Bagdad line.[17] The logical purpose for carrying out irrigation schemes close to railway lines was to increase agricultural production and the number of people residing in those areas. The direct benefits returning to the railway companies were visible in larger traffic in goods and personnel. Larger production would increase the revenue for the Porte from the tithe and other taxes. Again, increased revenue for the companies would lessen payments by the Ottoman Government, because of kilometric guarantees. To a distressed and indebted economy, any device aimed at lowering the debt burden ought to bring pleasure to the Sultan. Finally, one cannot lose sight of the primary objective of industrial nations, the acquisition of large amounts of raw materials for their expanding industries. Thus Earle says:

> Turkey-in-Asia, furthermore, was wealthy. It possessed vast resources of some of the most essentials of modern industry: minerals, fuel, lubricants, abrasives. Its deposits of oil alone were enough to arouse the cupidity of the Great Powers. Irrigation, it was believed, would accomplish wonders in the revival of the ancient fertility of Mesopotamia. By the development of the country's latent agricultural wealth and utilization of its industrial potentialities, it was anticipated that the Ottoman Empire would prove a valuable source of essential raw materials, a satisfactory market for finished products, and a rich field for the investment of capital. Economically, the territory served by the Bagdad Railway was one of the most important undeveloped regions of the world.[18]

Hence, while all interests involved were well served, the Foreign Powers, and particularly Germany, set an example. Though limited projects were advanced, it was hoped that relations with the Porte and the Ottoman citizens could be improved. For, while showing that they were serving the Ottoman Empire, they were advancing their own.[19] This was a calculated long-run gain.

The role of the Public Debt Administration in contributing to the economic welfare of the Ottoman economy should not be minimized.

> The Public Debt Administration were not unaware that the payment of railway subsidies would materially increase the amount of the imperial debt and mortgage certain of the imperial revenues. But they were confident that railways would be a powerful stimulant to economic prosperity in Turkey and would ultimately increase the revenues of the Government by an amount in excess of the amount of the subsidies. They believed that generous initial expenditures in a worthwhile enterprise might yield generous final returns . . . If the Public Debt Administration were actuated by self-interest, at least it was intelligent and far-sighted self-interest.[20]

2. *The Revenue Indicator*

In lieu of, or in addition to, computing the difference between the land cultivated before and after the railway age, a second method may be useful. Fluctuations in the revenue column of the Turkish budget may be used as another indicator.[21] During the period under consideration, increases in revenue to the Porte were principally due to absolute increases in tithes[22] and in other taxes connected with expanded agricultural production.

> A striking indication of the benefits conferred by the railway is given by the returns of the tithes collected by the Ottoman Public Debt, which in certain parts near the line yield five or six times the amount collected before the railway was built. It is not that population has appreciably increased; on the contrary the inhabitants of districts near the railway are always the first to be mobilized in time of war.[23]

Though no one can deny that railroads were principally responsible for larger production, other factors have to be accounted for. These factors may have been prompted by land reforms, such as the Vakuf reforms, or by changes in taxes, dues, and tariffs. Therefore, to depend solely on the revenue indicator as closely related to agricultural development due to railways may appear an enlightening abstraction, but is instead a misleading one.

In the first place, Ottoman budgets, even when available, were not always accurate. Not until the twentieth century did they become more dependable. Secondly, not all expansion in land use could be attributed to the railroad. Population increases normally call for a more intensive and extensive use of land. However, the recurrence of wars, among other things, limited population expansion in Turkey and undermines it as a factor in agricultural increase.

Thirdly, a good portion of the increase in revenue was due to an improved, better administration of the collection of taxes by the Public Debt Administration.[24]

> For twenty years subsequent to 1888 the Council assumed this function whenever a new concession was granted by the Government. By the year 1907 this function of intermediary between the concessionaire and the Government was being fulfilled for the following railway enterprises: Salonica-Constantinople (since 1894); Salonica-Monastir (since 1892); Smyrna-Cassaba and extensions (since 1894); Haidar Pasha-Angona and Eski Shehr-Konia (since 1888 for the former, 1893 for the latter); Bagdad (since 1903 for the first section, since 1908 for the second and third); Damascus-Hama and extensions (since 1897).[25]

It was not until 1888, however, that the Public Debt Administration began its role as an intermediary between the Porte and the various railway companies which had been assigned minimum returns by the respective concessions.[26]

3. *The Export Indicator*

As has been stated, railway development rendered great assistance to increased agricultural production. But without foreign markets to absorb the surplus, it would have been idle to produce it. Therefore, a good indicator which tends to show the extent of increased agricultural production in Turkey is the export sector. Statistics on Turkish exports to foreign countries were fairly reliable. While Turkish customs houses kept a good record of Turkey's exports, particularly in the twentieth century, even more reliable and accurate figures could be obtained from the customs houses of foreign countries dealing with Turkey. For example, Britain kept a good record of her trade relations with the Ottoman Empire.[27]

The figures in the following tables[28] are self explanatory. Although Turkish exports to Britain were shown in 1911-1912 to have risen slightly over those of 1900-1901 in absolute terms, they declined in relative terms. But the value of all exports from Turkey went up from £13,206,600 to £21,902,727. While total revenue from exports almost doubled, fluctuations in prices were not recorded. This presents a major drawback to this approach. Unless an intensive study is made of this problem to demonstrate the changes in the price level, no adequate results could be hoped for.

In 1914, the figures for foreign trade totalled approximately $175,000,000 for imports and $100,000,000 for exports.[29]

E. *Other Gains*

On the heels of railway development, extensive attempts were made by foreign investors to make use of privileges granted in conjunction with railway development.[30] These were restricted to mineral and agricultural resources and to improvements in docks, harbors, ports, etc. Mention of most of these developments has been made earlier. In fact, many of the rights and privileges for the exploitation of mineral resources and the establishment of hydroelectric power to generate electricity were granted by the Porte in its various railway concessions. In spite of the efforts made by foreign investors to take advantage of these concessions, obstructions often retarded and negated them nonetheless.

> As in all countries deficient in communications, fuel has been one of the great difficulties in Cilicia. There are several workable coal-mines in the district, but owing to the impossibility of obtaining concessions to exploit on reasonable terms, they remain untouched.[31]

The industrial growth made feasible by railway development was alluded to earlier: description of the prospering concerns of the Trypani Brothers and other industrial establishments which were fostered by railways, was presented earlier.[32] While bearing in mind that industrial and mining developments were limited in spite of railway facilities, the main factors for their retardation have already been discussed. To reiterate, however, the institutional background, the hesitation and often deliberately obstructive tactics of the Porte, and the availability of better investment opportunities elsewhere, negated these apparently handsome concessions. Besides, in the case of the Bagdad railway, it was hardly finished when war began and halted its successful operation. Time, as usual, was a dominant factor.

There is no doubt that immeasurable political and military gains were realized from railway development. A better transportation system enabled the Ottoman Government to exercise greater control over its far-flung provinces, and to maintain order and peace. The ability to mobilize troops and dispatch them to the front rapidly was becoming a necessity for national survival in an increasingly dynamic world.[33]

> From a military point of view, over and above the advantages of railway communication . . . , the opening up of the country has enabled the Ottoman Government to quell more than one insurrection in distant parts of the empire. In recent years this facility has been particularly valuable in the case of the Hidjaz, where there have been several rebellions. Moreover, the existence of railways renders possible a rapid mobilization of at least parts of the army.[34]

PART II

Economic Gains to Foreign Investors and to Foreign Powers

A. *Capital Investment*[35]

To begin with, foreign investment in the Turkish railways called for the transfer of large amounts of capital.[36] Unlike other types of capital movements which Turkey had experienced rather unpleasantly, these transfers were transformed into real capital: steel rails, locomotives, and different types of equipment, necessary for railroad construction and operation. The result became observable in the gradual increase in the exports of foreign countries to Turkey. Germany's role in supplying capital, for example, is evident in her export trade in the twentieth century, which will be taken up shortly. However, the total value of imports into Turkey increased from £21,124,000 in 1900-1901 to £39,800,000. A portion of the increase in imports went for consumers' goods, made possible by increased exports of agricultural products resulting from railroad facilities and from loans. Therefore, trade relations improved immensely between Turkey and the foreign countries. The gains are indicated in the value of goods exported and imported into Turkey which, in large part, resulted from railroad transportation.

In many instances, the Porte had to float bonds on foreign markets in order to provide capital for railway development. Bond flotation was carried out by various foreign companies, mostly by banks and brokers. Collection of imperial revenues and payment of these loans were left in the hands of the Public Debt Administration, which provided good security.[37]

In conjunction with the transfer of capital, foreign technical personnel were needed to assist in railway development. Also, additional investment in enterprises closely or even remotely connected with railways became important.[38]

It should not be forgotten that the abundance of capital in the industrial nations of Europe made it essential for European entrepreneurs to seek investment opportunities all over the world, including Turkey. Although investments in the United States and in Latin America were more remunerative and more secure, political motivations and long run indirect benefits weighed heavily in some of the decisions to invest in the Ottoman Empire.

B. *Turco-German and Turco-United States Trade Relations*

For the sake of illustration, a brief comparative study is presented of German-Turkish and United States-Turkish trade relations since the development of railroads in Turkey. The object of this study is to compare the change in trade relations between the two pairs and bring out the impact of railway development. In effect, this involves two extremes: in the first case, countries like Germany shared in and benefited from actual railway construction and its aftermath; in the second instance, countries remotely connected with railways in Turkey, such as the United States, benefited indirectly from railway transportation, and made possible greater volume of imports, as will be demonstrated later.

In Turco-German trade relations, the Germans showed more eagerness and greater activity than their predecessors and competitors, the British and the French, in carving out a sphere of influence in Turkey.[39] By the end of the nineteenth century, Germany had emerged as a great industrial power. Backed by an aggressive commercial and financial policy, she sought a network of markets for her industrial products, as well as for raw materials.[40] The construction of railways provided the first stepping stone in a series of designs for a larger economic penetration. Steel and iron rails, locomotives, coal, machinery and railroad equipment, and consumers' goods were among the major items on the export list from Germany to the Ottoman Empire. Imports of raw materials had also multiplied greatly. Note that trade figures between 1900 and 1912 showed a marked increase in exports and imports. For 1900-1901: Exports: £534,300; 1912: £4,045,000 or for 1900-1901: Imports: £583,000; 1912; £4,636,-000.

True, this is a general and incomplete picture, but it is indicative of a rising trend. Lack of substantial information makes it difficult to itemize the major articles for import and export. Although these figures are comprehensive, German exports to Turkey during this period primarily include manufactured goods, consumers goods, railroad equipment, but very little capital machinery. Imports from Turkey were principally agricultural food products and raw materials.

A look at trade relations between the United States and the Ottoman Empire between 1850 and 1914 shows a steady improvement. Total trade has risen from $596,626 in 1850 to $17,514,558 in 1914. When further itemized, the United States exports to Turkey in 1850 amounted to $204,397, while her imports in the same year amounted to $801,023.[41] But in 1914, the United States exports to Turkey amounted to $3,328,519,[42] while her imports rose to the phenomenal figure of $20,843,077. In the previous year, that is, in 1913, United States imports had attained their high of the whole sixty-three year period, totaling $22,159,285. It must be remembered that increased trade between the two nations did not come at the expense of other nations, but was a part of a general increase in absolute terms. Another reminder of importance is that price fluctuations must also be accounted for.[43]

Undoubtedly, much of this trade expansion could be directly attributed to railway development. The increased demand for raw materials in the United States made it incumbent upon the Ottoman Empire to increase its agricultural production and improve its means of transportation. As indicated by Gordon, the United States exported manufactured products to Turkey, mostly consumers' goods. Shipments of railway equipment, machinery, locomotives, steel, and other such items connected with railway construction and operation did not figure in the trade.

This leads to the conclusion that the United States benefited immeasurably from railway transportation in Turkey and contributed indirectly to the further expansion of railways, since she provided increasingly larger revenues to the Ottoman Empire from her purchase of raw materials.

C. *Conclusion*

Railway development, as has been observed, extended over a relatively long period of time. To construct and operate the railroads, foreign capital and technical personnel had to be imported at a high cost to the Porte. However, the presence of the railroad network proved to be a boon both for the Ottomans and for foreigners. Since only minor concomitant investments in industries and in mining were carried out, investment in railroad transportation was lopsided and had limited consequences. The improved means of transportation resulted mostly in agricultural expansion and benefited those connected with it. The continued existence of institutional problems, the fear of foreign industrialization, and the attitude towards reform and improvement confined the benefits of railroad communication to what has been shown. In order to demonstrate further how railroads in Turkey produced limited results, we turn next to a comparative study which, it is hoped, will expand and clarify some of the points raised in this chapter.

CHAPTER IV

Railroad Development in Great Britain, the United States, Tzarist Russia, and Turkey: A Comparative Study[1]

A. *Introduction*

In order to present a clearer picture of railroad development in the Ottoman Empire, it may be enlightening to present a brief comparative study. Contrasting a number of essential points may bring into focus certain aspects which may not have been clarified earlier. Besides, the comparative study has the added advantage of bringing into sharper focus certain corollary issues, such as the consequences of railway development in general and the way it affected the destiny of each country involved.

For the purpose of this study, only a couple of countries besides Turkey have been selected. Additional countries, if included, could lend heavier support to the advantages of the comparative study, but the choice of two countries should suffice for our purpose; additional pertinent information on other countries will be presented where useful.

The two countries of our choice are the United States and Great Britain. The latter provides an example of a country which was relatively advanced in industrial production when railway development took roots. The former was primarily agricultural when it embarked on railroad development, and in that respect, very much like the Ottoman Empire. In other respects, they were miles apart: their economic, political and social organizations and institutions were completely different.

Finally, time as usual, presented a dilemma. Since railroad development was started in Turkey in the eighteen-sixties, while it began three decades before this date in both Great Britain and the United States, Turkey had an advantage: it could use machinery that had already been tested, applied, and improved. In addition, the benefits that could be realized from railroads were known. But it is not only the actual time that is important; it is the whole setting of each country in time. Hence the answer to the paradox that railways in Turkey did not go far enough to produce fast change, as they did in Great Britain and the United States, though they appeared on the Turkish scene three decades later. Railway development, if examined in differing stages of development, regardless of chronological time, yields different results.

B. *The Background to Railroads*

Britain, endowed with several criss-crossing rivers, had found it convenient to construct canals as early as the mid-eighteenth century. Their presence helped her launch a new era in industrial development. Assisted by a flat country, the building costs of canals were fairly inexpensive. Within three decades, the whole country was linked with waterways, making it possible to lower transport costs. "As early as 1760 the Worsely Canal had reduced the price of coal in Manchester by 50 per cent."[2]

Therefore, the arrival of railroads in the eighteen twenties and thirties faced opposition from canal companies whose interests were endangered by the new competitor. It was only when railway transportation costs were further reduced and railways had established their usefulness that the British Government as well as the public accepted them and lent them assistance. In the first half of the nineteenth century, Britain was entering the embryonic stage of industrialization. With the help of the railway boom of the 1830's and 1840's, she advanced to industrial maturity very quickly.

Canal construction in the United States, however, followed expensive road building in the turnpike era on the Eastern seaboard, home of the early settlers. A canal system seemed promising at the turn of the nineteenth century, in the light of the earlier British experience with them. It seemed not unreasonable to believe that a canal system, if carried out, would afford inexpensive transportation, reach previously inaccessible areas, and bring about expanded economic activity with benefits to the community. When the Erie Canal was built (1817-1825) and operated with financial success, such optimism seemed to be well founded. But with the physical features and the natural waterways of the young Republic of the nineteenth century, no one pattern of canal construction seemed feasible. Therefore, three major patterns emerged: East of the Appalachians, in those states bordering on the Atlantic sea coast from Maine to Virginia, the need was for canals to improve the transportation between the upcountry and the tidewater, and from one river basin to an adjacent one. The Cumberland and Oxford Canal in Maine (1827-1870's) was an excellent example of the first, and the Delaware and Hudson (one of the Anthracite Canals) filled the second need. In helping to transport this new fuel, anthracite, from Philadelphia to New York, the Delaware and Hudson Canal rendered a valuable service.

The second group was designed to connect the Atlantic states with the Ohio River Valley and the Great Lakes. Both the James River and Kanawha Canal and the Chesapeake and Ohio Canal were intended to be constructed across the Appalachians to the Ohio river, but neither succeeded in crossing the mountains, The Pennsylvania canal system the "Main Line" constructed in 1826-1834 did connect Philadelphia and Pittsburgh, but it was forced to cross a hundred mile stretch of the Appalachians by an inclined railway. The railway and the excessive number of locks required raised the cost of freight considerably. Thus the most successful of all was the Erie Canal, built between 1817 and 1825. It connected Albany with Buffalo by a low level route and led to a reduction of approximately 90% in the cost of transporting goods between the two cities, thus making it possible to haul bulky products from the interior to the East and bring manufactured articles to the West.

In the midwestern states of Ohio, Indiana, and Illinois, the planning of canals had for its major objective the connection of the Ohio-Mississippi river system with the Great Lakes. One of these, the Ohio and Erie Canal, went into operation in 1823. However, most of the canals built in the old Northwest were completed so late as to be in immediate competition with railways, a factor which prevented their financial success. Their impact, in fact, lay more in the initiation of new enterprises than in their financial success as transportation facilities.

In Turkey, the nature of the physical features and the absence of significant waterways would have meant high expenses for canal construction and operation. The presence of the high rugged plateau in the Anatolian region would have rendered canal construction almost impossible. In order to connect this plateau with the sea ports, many locks would have been needed, requiring additional operating costs to run them. Nor were most of the other areas within the Ottoman Empire productive enough at the time to justify the construction of canals. Thus there was no sense in constructing canals, or in improving or even building roads in Turkey, as long as railways, whose effectiveness had been tested, could transport all types of traffic at a faster rate and at lower costs. Therefore, when the railroad companies appeared on the scene, they did not have to confront competition from canal or road companies. There was no resistance of note on this front, although railroad interests often provided keen competition amongst themselves. A company or a foreign power that did not reach an agreement with the Porte tried to make it difficult for those in the Sultan's favor, and vice-versa.

C. *Construction and Operation of the Railway System*

1. *Resources and methods of financing*

The presence of iron and coal in close proximity, the availability of local engineers and businessmen, and the abundance of local skills and capital all combined to simplify the task of railway development in industrialized Britain. Rolling stock; locomotives, machinery and wheels; railroad rails; and sundry railway equipment were domestically produced. Local railway companies had only these kinds of problems to cope with: competing for royal sanction, appeasing or fighting canal and coal companies, and warding off railway competition in their own area of service. Needless to say, railway development in Britain in its early stages had to pass through a period of trial and error, starting with short lines where traffic was heaviest and a reasonable rate of return assured, and then consolidating. But capital was abundant in Britain; the investors had only to be convinced of the profitability of railways over other investments.

In the United States,[3] corporations were chartered to develop railway lines, and they demanded large quantities of capital and raw materials. In their formative stage, railway companies had to import iron and steel rails, locomotives, and other needed machinery from Britain. Even capital shortages were experienced. In spite of increasing flotation of bonds and stocks on the stock markets, the role of the small investors (the farmer, the professional, the businessman and the small manufacturer) became indispensable. The government (national, state and local) also lent its financial support. In some instances, in Georgia and in Virginia, where private capital was not forthcoming, the state owned and operated the railway. In addition, stocks and bonds were floated in European markets.

> American railroad securities found at least a limited sale in London before 1850, and the bonds of American states marketed abroad helped to provide capital for railroad financing.[4]

In the railway development of the Ottoman Empire, workers and timber were provided locally. Everything else had to be imported, including the technical personnel. This important factor is enough in itself to explain the high cost of construction and operation, and the consequent high transport charges. An equally important factor stems from the fact that some of the foreign investors owned the railway lines under concessions, with guaranteed fixed profits. Still another important reason for high transport charges is the lack of traffic, both in goods and in persons. The financial, economic, social, political, and military situation in the Ottoman Empire necessitated the unusually high interest and amortization charges involved in the necessary flotation of capital issues on the European markets.

2. *Role of the Government*

Judging by the large number of Railway Acts passed by the British Parliament in the 1830's and 1840's,[5] one may conclude that the British Government was favorable to railway development in legislation. Though this period is characterized as one of uncertainty for the railways, opposition by canal and road companies during this period was largely unsuccessful. Their vested interests were threatened and weakened, but they could not obstruct the sweeping move towards railways. At that early stage of development, no attempt was made by Parliament to regulate or guide the new enterprise.[6] As a result, much useless or purely competitive construction occurred. This was a period of trial and error for the railways, and mistakes and duplications were inevitable.

In the United States, the federal, state, and local governments were not passive in railway development. Under a temporary law passed in 1824, federal engineers were enlisted from West Point to make railroad surveys at the expense of the government.

> More important in monetary terms was the provision made by Congress, 1830-1843, for reduction of the tariff duties on iron used in railroad construction.[7]

Federal land grants to railway companies began in 1850, but significant loans for railroad construction were not furnished until after the Civil War.

Instead, the state and local governments contributed heavily prior to the Civil War. Charters, easily secured from state legislatures, contained sweeping privileges as regards free land grants and few restraints on the form and amount of securities issued. In the South, in Virginia and Georgia, where private capital was not forthcoming, railroads were financed largely by the state. Tersely expressed:

> The state government contributed to the rapid growth of the railroad net 1. by putting liberal provisions in railroad charters, 2. by actually building railroads, and 3. by supplying needed money and credit for private construction.[8]

In the Ottoman Empire it was a different story. Being more independent in his power, the Sultan could and did go further than the Government of the United States. Driven by the pressing need for transportation, the Sultan showed no signs of reluctance or passivity in making sacrifices. He mortgaged his possessions and his revenues for years to follow in order to pay for the high costs of railways. Despite its state of indebtedness and the reign of confusion, the Turkish Government did everything possible to assist in railroad development, hoping to maintain if not save the empire. The following is not an exhaustive but certainly a lengthy list of the important facilitations offered, often included in the concessions granted by the Porte.[9] (a)

Generous land grants and other privileges: Free land for right of way was usually granted for quarries and sand pits along the route of construction; freedom from rental costs was granted; the rights to establish and operate tile and brick works, to work mines within a zone usually twenty kilometres on either side of the line; and to carry archeological research for works of art within the area of construction were guaranteed. Railway companies were permitted to cut wood from the state forests without compensation. (b) Rights to facilities connected with railways: railway companies were often given rights to construct and own, at their expense, harbors, docks, quays, warehouses, and whatever was deemed necessary to help in railway construction. For example, the Bagdad Railway Company was given navigation and port rights in Mesopotamia. The Smyrna-Aidin Company built its own pier in Smyrna. (c) Duty-free imports: Taxes and duties were suspended on materials needed for railway development. For instance, iron and steel rails and coal were exempt from customs duties and from any local taxes. Even the land, the capital, and the revenue of railway companies were tax-free during the period of the concession. (d) Financing: Perhaps most important of all was the help offered by the Turkish Government in the form of kilometric guarantees to meet the costs of construction and operation. Funds were usually raised in European capitals through the flotation of securities, which were guaranteed by the revenue of certain districts through which the railways passed. The presence of the Public Debt Administration was instrumental in administering and collecting these revenues and thereby in lending security to the investors. In brief, the Porte, at least on paper, lent its full and unquestionable support.

In contrast to the United States, Great Britain, and Turkey, railway development in France took a completely different course, once a few short lines were constructed between 1823 and 1832.[10] In 1833, a law was enacted for the purpose of appropriating funds for planning a network of railroads. Nine years later, in 1842, a bill was introduced. It subsequently became law, authorizing such a network. It laid down rules for its construction, but there were many changes in French policy—financing, concessions, and supervision by the Government.[11]

3. *Extent of Development*

If a period of fifty to sixty years (roughly between 1860 and 1914 for Turkey) is considered adequate to compare the extent of railway development in Britain, the United States, and Turkey, the following information is relevant.

In the United Kingdom—England, Wales, Scotland and Ireland, possessing an area of 121,136 square miles (with Northern Ireland, only 94,000 square miles)—the railroad mileage reads as follows: Until 1830, only fifty-one miles of railway were opened to traffic.[12] By 1848, the total ran up to 5,000 miles or 8,000 kilometres. In 1865, seventy-eight companies owned and controlled 11,451 miles. Around 18,000 route miles were attained by 1880. In the following decade, about 2,000 more miles were added. Thus the total of railroad mileage operated in the 1890's amounted to about 20,000 miles, or roughly 32,400 kilometres. The gauge adopted for the railway track was four feet, eight-and-a-half inches. (4ft. 8½in.).

The United States of the nineteenth century possessed an area of 3,022,000 square miles. In 1830, the total railroad mileage was only 73 miles. By 1850 it increased to 8,879 miles; in 1870, it was 52,885 miles; in 1880, 93,671 miles and by 1900, it had climbed to 163,581 miles, or 263,365 kilometres. The peak was not reached until the 1930's, however, when the total railroad mileage climbed to a total of 252,836 miles. Though various gauges for railway tracks were used, the four-feet-eight-and-a-half inches was most common. Later, the whole system was standardized.

In an area of 913,000 square miles, about ten times that of Great Britain and one-third that of the United States, Turkey, on the eve of the war, had a meagre 5,252 kilometres of railway. By 1900, she had about 4500 kilometres. This leads to the obvious conclusion that even after fifty years of railway investment, Turkey remained deficient in adequate means of transportation. In fact, the skeleton of railway lines had not even been completed by World War I. Most of the Turkish lines connected commercial lines, with one line track. In the United States, a good deal of the lines were double tracks and fillings. This increase in the density of the network comes from and is indicative of prosperity.[13]

4. *Consequences of railway development*

The first railway lines in Britain are usually referred to as the 'coal-lines' because they specialized in transporting coal. For example, the Act of 1830 permitted the construction of the Leicester and Swannington coal line. It is needless to emphasize the role of coal for the British industries, as well as for export.

When railroads began to make headway in Britain, the country had already become the industrial centre of the world. Railways transported new material and foodstuffs to the interior and carried manufactured goods to the ports for export overseas. The process, though subject to fluctuation, was continuous: the railway cars were filled on both journeys, rendering railway investment quite remunerative. With the traffic in persons also exceeding all expectations, transport costs were further reduced. As they lowered, the export price of British commodities on the world markets was also reduced. Besides, the costs of raw materials and foodstuffs going into the interior helped to maintain low wages and a high real income. Hence, the double impact of raw materials and manufactured goods could not be ignored in bringing about lower costs of production and lower sales costs on manufactured products. In effect, lower transportation costs helped Britain in her competition on the world markets, as newly rising industrial powers began to market competitive goods in areas where Britain held some monopoly.

In the case of Britain, railways were complementary to the existing waterways. They did not hold the principal role, as in the case of the Ottoman Empire. They helped industrial expansion, encouraged population movements, and aided in tapping resources which were inaccessible to waterways.

In the financial market, railway investment gradually made its impact on the British Stock Market. Millions of pounds were invested in railway stocks and bonds, many times spurting booms or causing depressions.

Railway construction in the United States generally preceded the growth in population and industrialization. Therefore, expected direct returns on railway investments were delayed. However, after the Civil War, a marked increase was felt in both industrialization and population. Development in the former centered in the North, as the South continued to be predominantly agricultural. Thus, its benefits were limited since railway penetration was late.

Industrial and agricultural development in the United States was further enhanced in the 1850's, however, by the establishment of regular railroad schedules, which made possible a consistent flow of raw materials to the factory and of manufactured items from it. The consolidation of short lines into a network was effected during this period and was instrumental in lowering costs and helping along the growth of traffic.

With a spreading railway network, transport costs were therefore reduced. Agriculture was commercialized. Development in industries and in mining, assisted by growing concurrent institutions, proceeded at a rapid pace, leading to the expansion of internal and external trade. Thus, regularity of transportation made continued production possible at lower costs, leading in turn to a reduction in the price of manufactured items.

Reference was made earlier to the trade relations between Turkey and the United States, confirming that railways in the Ottoman Empire provided gradually increasing quantities of needed raw material in the United States. One could further add that railways in this country transported the raw materials to their proper destination and carried light manufactured goods for export to Turkey.

What, perhaps, had contributed to and magnified the role of railways in the United States is the fact that concurrent industrial and financial institutions, population growth, and favorable government legislation all interacted to give impetus to general economic growth. Bolino adds:

> Railroad finance encouraged the use of the corporation, fostered the development of the stock exchanges, and led to a rationalization of investment banking. Finance capitalism was born with the corporation and nurtured on the battleground on railroad finance. All the important institutions of this phase of capitalism-stock-exchanges, insurance companies, finance corporations and investment banks—developed in the era of railroad expansion.[14]

As to the extent of railway development in Turkey, it was confined and plagued by shortages of all kinds.[15] Limited railway facilities retarded internal development. The railway lines had different gauges, owned and operated by different groups who did not favor conjunctions between their lines. These group kept up keen competition amongst themselves, and the result was that further facilitations were obstructed.

Since Turkey continued to be predominantly agricultural until World War I, the best service rendered by railroads was the commercialization of agricultural products: an increase in the shift from subsistence to commercial farming. Passenger traffic continued to be light because the Ottoman citizen received a very small income and could ill afford the high cost of travel.[16]

However, the basic problem confronting agricultural communities in general, and Turkey in particular, is the fact that in an agricultural community, production follows a seasonal pattern, which in turn affects the transportation system.[17] The railways would be active during the period of harvest and slack during the rest of the year. In the case of the Ottoman Empire, the lack of proper storage facilities meant that agricultural products had to be transported at harvest time. Going to the ports, cars would be loaded, and returning, empty. The process was costly to operate and could only be resolved in higher costs. But agricultural production has a ceiling and is subject also to the law of diminishing returns.

Then, imported consumers' goods were mainly consumed on the coastal areas, where the minority groups resided. Very small quantities were transported internally. Poverty, little economic activity, and non-industrialization meant low incomes to Ottomans and low revenues to railways. The scarcity of population in most areas traversed by railways and the restrictions on travel under Abdul Hamid were unfavorable as well.

In Germany, the railway system brought prosperity that helped the nation overcome its economic stagnation. Changes in old habits resulted. Above all, it fostered large-scale industrialization. In France, as well as in Britain, Germany, and the United States, railways helped the growth of industries, fostered mining, gave rise to institutions, and brought prosperity to agricultural and urban communities. In these countries, railways helped traffic all year round. It is true that railroads were subject to the impact of fluctuations, but they stood to prosper with prosperity and suffer with depressions. The same was true of Turkey, since the demand for her raw materials depended upon the industrial prosperity of Western nations.

D. *Turkey and Tzarist Russia*

In view of the interesting points of similarities and differences between Tzarist Russia and Turkey, a brief comparative discussion has its usefulness. The following examination strengthens the view that differences in the institutional backgrounds which act as a springboard are largely responsible for the rate of economic development. Specifically, countries like Russia and Turkey had to start at a lower level of economic development than most of the European countries.

Although railway development was begun in Russia in the 1830's, it was not until the 1880's that it played a major role in her large scale industrial development. The slow rate of development that followed the initial railways may be largely attributed to the presence of feudal institutions, which finally began to break down with the emancipation of the serfs in 1861. The freed serfs were allowed to purchase land from the lords. Since they did not have any money, however, they bought land on credit, with the Russian Government lending a helping hand in the transaction. Thus the freed serfs, i.e., the new peasants, were indebted to both the government and to the lords. The partial payment received by the lords from the government was in the form of bonds. But the lords had been previously in debt to their government, and therefore this process of transferring assets left no liquidity in the hands of either the peasants or the lords.

> The lords were heavily in debt in 1861. In the past they had borrowed money from the state on the security of their serfs, and their estates were mortgaged for a large part of their value. A considerable part of the redemption payments was absorbed by the liquidation of these debts; much of the remainder was squandered in extravagant living, in unwise investments, or in unprofitable improvements. Lords, like serfs, were medieval in their psychology, quite unqualified to keep their place in a more modern society. Their place and privileges had in the past been assured them

by custom. When they had to enter into a system of contract, they soon betrayed their inexperience and their poor judgment.[18]

As a consequence, not much money was available to the public for use in investment. This explains in large part why the Russian Government had to carry the burden of industrialization, including railway development.

Other problems connected with agriculture had to do with the system of land tenure in the communal village, which lessened the opportunities of the villagers to save and possibly to reinvest, was that the owners of the fertile land had to pay the taxes of the less fortunate who owned poorer lands.[19] This was so because the communal village was assessed a certain amount of taxes as a whole, with the large burden falling on those who produced most. As a result, not much money was left for savings and investment.

In Turkey, the *millet* system which gave rise to social rigidities and prevented national assimilation, was also one of the factors in the low level of economic deveolpment. The profits which were reaped by the non-Muslim *millets* were either invested abroad or left in liquid form, not reinvested locally. With respect to the Muslims, the majority of whom were peasants and small landholders, they produced mostly for local consumption. The tax burden was onerous. When, in the latter part of the nineteenth century, agricultural production was increased, so were taxes. But the profit realized in this expansion was squandered on consumers' goods and not used for investment purposes.

In Russia, as well as in Turkey, the main motive for industrial development lay in military as well as in political needs. In both instances, economic development was largely a function of military and political motivations, and therefore acquired a rather peculiar character. It was jerky and did not sustain a drive. Russia's never-ending expansionist plans in the direction of the Balkans and towards Constantinople became strongly associated with industrial development, including a network of railway communication. Furthermore, Russia feared for the loss of Siberia and promoted the Trans-Siberian railway in the

1880's. In the same vein, Turkey promoted railway construction in order to further centralize the authority of the Porte and maintain the integrity of her empire.

In both countries, shortages of capital and technical labor necessitated their importation at high cost from more advanced European communities. However, Russia developed an edge over Turkey in this respect.

Firstly, Russian entrepreneurs gained and put to use the new ideas, attitudes, and aspirations essential for industrial development. Assisted by their government, they even went so far as to concentrate on heavy industries. Perhaps the geographical position of Russia, which rendered difficult the transportation of bulky material into the interior, contributed to this policy. For one thing, many of the Russian ports in the North Sea are not usable for several months of the year, nor are the many rivers that flow into them because of cold weather. Besides, the large expanses of Siberia are arid and have no waterways of significance. In order consistently to provide needed goods it was essential to construct factories in the interior and provide a transportation system that could be useful all year round. In Turkey's case, Ottoman groups were less amenable towards acquiring these new economic ideas and developing new attitudes. The whole institutional background was unfavorable; and industrial development lagged.

Secondly, the role of the Russian Government was more active than Turkey's in providing capital for industrial development, including railways. Attempting to raise capital abroad to help finance Russia's industrial growth, the Russian Government did not encounter the same difficulties then being experienced by the Porte. Political reasons helped the Russians to raise the needed capital in French markets, for the French needed a strong ally in the East against Germany.

By providing capital for industrialization, the Russian Government filled the function of industrial banks. The Russian Government, on October 1, 1900, owned and operated 20,000 miles of railways out of a network of 34,485 miles (including 1,721 miles in Finland).[20] On January 1, 1913, Russia had 46,573 miles of railways opened to traffic, with 33,928 miles belonging to and worked by the Government.

In Turkey, the Government provided kilometric guarantees and limited its assistance to railways. Turkey's lone ownership was of the Hejaz line. By 1914, the extent of railway development was limited to 5,252 kilometres, mostly owned and operated by foreign companies. It may be added that Turkey's large foreign debt prevented her from embarking upon any industrial policy that may have been fomenting. Owned and operated mostly by foreign capitalists, the banks in Turkey played a significant part in fulfilling the functions of commercial banks, but seldom those of the industrial banks. Their continued rivalries frustrated any concerted effort towards Turkish industrial development.

Internally in both Turkey and Russia, economic development produced a drain on the economy, calling for reform. New measures of reform and taxation had to be carried out. Larger revenues to the Russian Government were redirected towards industrial development, but larger revenues in Turkey were used to pay the external debt and provide the miiltary with its needs.

Finally, railway development in Russia of the 19th century generated a greater economic activity than it did in Turkey. The endowment of natural resources, the strength of the institutional obstacles and many other pertinent factors were all more favorable to Russian than to Turkish development: hence the difference in the rate of growth in both countries.

E. *Conclusion*

The brief comparative study presented in this chapter points out the limited extent of railway development in the vast expanses of the Ottoman Empire, as compared with that of Britain, the United States, and Tzarist Russia. It confirms the opinion that the institutional background in Turkey confined the economic consequences of railway development. It also reveals that growth was stifled. As has been shown, the Porte invested large amounts of capital for kilometric guarantees, without the benefit of the economic development which would have alleviated the financial burden consequent upon railway investment.

No one can accuse the Ottoman Government of having failed to support railway investment in its country. In spite of Turkey's indebtedness, the Sultan went ahead, mortgaging her resources in the hope of holding the empire intact and expanding her agricultural wealth. By 1914, the Porte was still paying large amounts of money for the kilometric guarantees it had granted in connection with its concessions to railway investors.

In the following chapter, an attempt will be made to evaluate this investment in railways, sum up its limited impact upon the economy, and examine the alternatives open to the Ottoman Empire.

CHAPTER V

Evaluation and Conclusion

A. *Introduction*

It has been shown that by the mid-nineteenth century, Turkey was sadly deficient in her internal means of transportation. Her institutions were depicted as backward; her economy, relative to those of European countries, undeveloped; and her government corrupt, autocratic and inefficient. A state of discontent and dissatisfaction prevailed. The Crimean War then placed the empire into severe financial straits and large-scale borrowing ensued. The extragavant Sultan Abdul Aziz thought he could save the empire through borrowing and the theoretical initiation of a policy of economic development. In both instances, he failed. Borrowing continued until Turkey defaulted on her payments in 1875, and then was resumed under Abdul Hamid. Railways were started as a first step to general development, but when superficial rather than fundamental changes proved to be all that was forthcoming, all hopes for strength and greatness faded away.

The lopsided development in railways did lead to increased economic activity. But it served primarily the agricultural endeavors for which the empire was then most suited, although railway investment also fitted the purposes of foreign investors and the Foreign Powers. While promoting other functions, railway development could therefore produce no more than a slow rate of economic growth, a much slower rate than in any of the European nations, the United States, or Japan. Hence the conclusion is inevitable that governmental shortcomings accompanied railway development, insofar as it failed to produce long needed social, economic, and political changes.

The attention of the Sublime Porte was absorbed so intensely in the military and the political aspects of national survival and the maintenance of the integrity of the empire that inadequate attention was given to those aspects pertaining to the economy. Much of the emphasis that the Porte laid in the economic sphere was in the direction of railways. However, even capital involved in railway expansion could have been used in other more promising ways, which might have changed the destiny of the empire.

Therefore, in view of the costs involved and the limited development that ensued, it is important to enquire into the reasons that had led to the emphasis on railway development. Was it not possible for the Porte to encourage concurrent industrialization, or even pursue a different course than the one adopted? To this line of enquiry this chapter is devoted.

B. *Evaluating Railroad Development*

In the railroad development of Turkey, one has to contend with three major factions, each with varying interests and objectives: the Ottoman Government, the foreign investors, and the foreign governments. The Porte was interested in possessing an adequate means of transportation. But political and military, as well as economic, factors weighed heavily in the Porte's decision in favor of railways. As will be shown, the price paid was exorbitant. The foreign investors, on the other hand, were interested primarily in the economic aspects of their investment, namely, in a high and secure rate of profit. This was especially true in the early stages of railways. The expectation of a high rate of return motivated the construction of the Smyrna-Aidin line without any guarantees. However, this is not to be construed as meaning that later investors were not actuated by the profit motive, whether in railways or in related concessions, but rather that political and military factors began to assume greater importance after the 1880's. Finally, foreign governments became more concerned with railways and railway companies. The German government supported those German investors who were anxious to construct the Bagdad line. Political and military considerations in this instance were perhaps adjudged of equal importance to the economic.

In applying our criteria for evaluating railway development discussed earlier, first let us examine its impact on the first two groups, Turkey and the foreign investors. In the last two chapters, emphasis was laid on the economic and non-economic benefits realized by Turkey. It was demonstrated that her gains were primarily in the agricultural and foreign trade sectors. The expansion in agriculture assisted by railroad development yielded substantial increases in revenues to the state, consisting mainly of tithes, taxes, and customs duties. As the foreign demand increased, farming was expanded and Ottoman citizens gained. But in spite of the increase in economic activity, the consequences to general economic development were not as large or as significant as they could have been. The truth is that railway development was carried out at such a high cost to the Ottoman Government that alternatives should have been considered.

The early investments in railways, were executed at no monetary cost to the Government of the Ottoman Empire, since no kilometric guarantees were involved. Railway lines were run in densely populated areas which abounded with opulent resources. They were rewarding on their own, but many of the later lines, constructed in thinly populated areas which often lacked natural wealth, were not profitable. In those instances, the political and military factors superseded the immediate economic gains. As no foreign investor was prepared to undertake an investment so insecure, apparently profitless, the Porte consented to grant railway concessions that carried kilometric guarantees covering operating costs and in some cases, construction costs. This was an appealing guarantee to railway investors. The question then became, how much of a guarantee to wrench from the Porte?

In order to have a better idea of some of the expenses incurred by the Ottoman Government, the following is a list of the amounts paid for railway concessions from 1889 to 1901. A complete summary of railway guarantees is not possible to construct. However, after 1901, it is known that there was continued spending for other lines, particularly the Bagdad line.

Year	Number of Kilometers	Amounts paid in Francs
1889	92	165,568
1890	116	135,614
1891	217	608,795
1892	340	2,000,409
1893	675	5,054,318
1894	876	6,769,545
1895	1,444	11,095,818
1896	1,906	14,785,523
1897	2,069	7,178,523
1898	2,269	16,466,955
1899	2,269	19,942,863
1900	2,269	17,958,170
1901	2,269	15,359,446[2]

C. *Foreign Investment in Railways Revisited*[3]

The strange situation in the Ottoman Empire which had invited foreign investors to plough money into railways has already been presented at length.[4] There remains to be discussed the world situation as far as investment opportunities are concerned.

Until 1875, when the Ottoman Government defaulted on its payments to foreign lenders, British and French capital flowed into the Ottoman Empire. A part of it went into what was believed to be a handsome reward in railways. After all, investors are generally interested in an annual return, and a high rate of profits, as well as any privilege or concession which might also be negotiated. But investment in railways had its peculiar difficulties.

> European promoters who had constructed lines in Turkey before 1875 underwent many difficulties with the Govern-

ment in the matter of tariffs, securities, bank accounts and protection of their property. The rude jolt which in 1875 shocked holders of the Government's securities, discouraged further the persons with capital already invested in railroads, as well as those who possessed ideas concerning future development of rail communications.[5]

Earlier, in 1873, the world economic panic had discouraged any new movement of capital from the European countries. But towards the end of the decade, world booms reinstated large capital flows. Two factors accounted for these flows: (a) their domestic securities provided only low yields at the time and (b) better opportunities became available in Australia, Canada, South America and the United States, where economic development was advancing at a rapid pace. The discoveries of gold and diamonds in South Africa opened new outlets for European investment.

Undaunted by the impropitious conditions in Turkey, France and Germany proceeded to expand their investments there after the eighteen eighties, while Britain hesitated, and finally decided to tap more profitable and secure regions. In their policy of investment expansion, France and Germany were encouraged by the establishment in 1881 of the Ottoman Public Debt Administration, whose primary role was to collect money for the foreign Bondholders. Indirectly, the Public Debt Administration sought to redeem lost confidence. Its role was instrumental in guaranteeing railway investment and promoting its success.

By 1914, of a total of 45 billion francs invested overseas, France had invested 3.3 billion in Turkey. Half a billion flowed into railway development.[6] Germany's investment in Turkey totaled 1.8 million Marks out of a total foreign investment of 23.5 billion Marks.[7] British long-term, publicly issued, capital stock investment in Turkey amounted to £24 million out of a grand total of overseas investment of £3,763.3 million.

The above figures tend to indicate that the ration of capital invested by Germany, Great Britain and France in the Ottoman Empire was a small percentage of their total overseas investment. In percentages, Germany and France invested about 7½ of their total investment in Turkey, while Britain invested only 0.7%. Out of these totals and those of other foreign investments, the amount invested in Turkey's railways in 1914 reached the large figure of $170,070,828.[8] In other words,

> Of the total debt, as it stood in 1914, about one-fifth had been put to productive use. Turkey had 5,252 kilometers of railroad, representing a nominal invested capital of approximately 45 million Turkish pounds; but at least a third of this mileage was built without expense to the government.[9]

D. *Alternatives to Railway Investment*

In order to complete our discussion of investment, the possible alternatives to railway investment must be considered. It is hoped that this discussion will shed more light on the Porte's decisions to invest in railways.

Perhaps an injustice is rendered to the Ottoman Empire by alleging that its ruling institution comprehended the full significance of industrial development in the West, and fully understood its prosperous economic consequences. It has never been made clear whether the Ottoman Government had economists who deliberated the problem of development, sketched a series of choices ranging from, say, textiles to railways, or that finally, of the many alternatives deliberated, railways received top priority. All the indications are, in fact, that there was only one obsession. The Porte seemed to confine its considerations to choosing one railway project over another, deciding which foreign investors were to be granted the concessions, and working out what was to be included in these concessions. Undeniably, railway development carried with it many assets. It could have gone a long way to maintain the integrity of the Ottoman Empire and produce economic prosperity. But if specialization in railways had its virtues, it certainly had its drawbacks as well.

At first glance it seems plausible that, considering the economic and political situation of the time, the Ottoman Empire did the best it could under the circumstances. The pressing need for adequate means of communication, the benefits realized from railway development, and the further rewards to be achieved—all these weighed heavily in favor of railways. But emphasizing railways to the neglect of other types of development, whether in industry or in government, carried with it certain disadvantages.

Turkey was in dire need of industries to produce goods to raise its standard of living and improve its material well-being. After shifting its financial resources to railways, the Porte could do little in other fields.

To reiterate, railway development led finally only to agricultural development, which was bound to reach a ceiling. Agriculture is an economic activity of a seasonal nature; railways could be run profitably for only about five months of the year. Slow progress in agricultural production without industrial development confined railway income and restricted growth in the economy. In other words, given Turkey's institutional background, agricultural production could not generate large enough incomes to create the economic activity that would eventually bring about industrialization and a higher standard of living.

One of the alternatives to the development of the Bagdad line was distinctly brought out by Fraser.

> If the Turkish Government could wipe out the Bagdad Convention and devote some of the money they propose wasting upon its fulfillment to formulating and executing a sound system of immigration of Moslems from foreign countries to Turkey, they would be embarking upon an enterprise that would give an almost immediate return in the shape of rents, taxes, railway receipts, customs dues, and increase in the population available for military duty. If they would set up in various districts depots for the exhibition of agricultural machinery, if they would demonstrate its use and encourage purchase by accepting payments by easy instalments, they would set free from daily labor large numbers of people who would then be available to open up ground that is now neglected.[10]

Alternatives to railway development are of a speculative nature and easily presented. They belong to the many "ifs" of the past. But cognizant of the dangers and limitations involved in every possible alternative opened to the Porte, we can only briefly sketch the following possibilities, which are neither exhaustive nor conclusive. (a) The Porte could have neglected its duties in the distant provinces and concentrated on the heartland. Instead of spending so much capital on armies and armaments needed to suppress rebellions and fight the little wars cropping up here and there in the Empire, why was it not spent on industrialization? However, the prestige element by itself, let alone the myriad ramifications involved in such a negative attitude, would have been detrimental to the power of the Sultan and what it stood for. This then takes us to the second but more palatable possibility, where a positive action is suggested by the Porte in regards to the distant provinces.

(b) Since railway development was costly and did not achieve much of what it had purported to do for example—to help maintain the integrity of the empire—why did not the Porte seek a different course? For example, why did not the Ottoman Government allow the provinces on the outer periphery, in Africa, Asia, and Europe, to become semi-independent, with close political and economic ties with the Porte; that is, create a looser federation which could have been stronger than a disorganized and a malfunctioning centralized empire? In that instance, money spent on the political and military machines could have been used for industrial purposes. As Toynbee and Kirkwood point out in the following quotation, the distant provinces were lost anyway, after World War I. Hence, such an alternative might have been a proper step in the right direction.

> In the first place those alien provinces—Tripoli-Benghazi in Africa, Albania and Macedonia in Europe, and the Arab provinces in Asia, not to speak of the nominal Ottoman suzerainty over Egypt and Bosnia-Herzegovina—were not lost once and for all, with a finality so patent that even the least impressionable Turkish "die-hard" could no longer seriously contemplate their recovery. Subjectively, this presented a crushing defeat, for the Turks had concentrated their energies for ten years on trying to retain these territories. In truth, however, her alien provinces had been a millstone round Turkey's neck ever since the breakdown of the indigenous Ottoman system under which they had furnished recruits for the Sultan's slave-household and fiefs for his free Muslim feudatories. It would have been vastly better for Turkey if she had let these provinces go without pouring out her blood and treasure to keep them; but that would have been too much to expect of human nature, and,

in the cutting of losses, 'better late than never.' After full allowance for the cost of the process, the sloughing off of these provinces was a net gain to the Turkish people and the Turkish state.[11]

(c) While pursuing (a) or preferably (b), the Ottoman Government could have had peace at a price that had its rewards. The money saved from the futile attempts to quell insurrections could have been used for a regional or a gradual overall development in the whole empire. For instance, the industrial development of Anatolia, the heartland of the empire, could have been achieved, with far-reaching consequences.

At this juncture, it may be asked, why did none of the Sultans in the nineteenth century execute an industrialization scheme similar to that which was carried out by Muhammad Ali of Egypt, in the 1830's? For, like the Ottoman Empire, Egypt in the 19th century (roughly 1808-1881) was subject to a capitulatory regime which gave special rights and privileges to foreigners. She also had her tariffs fixed by conventions: they could not be altered by any one party without the unanimous consent of the powers concerned. Besides, Egypt got involved in financial borrowing and eventually fell victim to great international economic and financial pressures.

Now, it may be recalled that some industrialization in Egypt took place during a few years in the the 1830's. But then, in the early 1840's, an agreement was reached between the Great Powers and the Porte, which conferred the hereditary pashalik upon Muhammad Ali and his descendants. After that, Muhammad Ali paid great attention to the armed forces, and the incentive for industrialization gradually faded away. Furthermore, foreign competition protected by the capitulations was detrimental to local industries.

How then was industrialization possible in a country as backward as Egypt? Prof. Issawi stresses the point that Muhammad Ali was temporarily favored by a period of political independence which gave him a breathing spell to plan and execute his industrial schemes. But this political autonomy was only one of the prerequisites for industrialization.

In brief, Mohammad Ali was trying to carry out a program of forced industrialization. His success was due primarily to the administrative protection that he gave to his infant industries, which did not, however, outlive that protection. The capital required for establishing those industries was obtained from the profits of his monopoly of internal and export trade, from taxation and forced loans, and the losses of industrial enterprises were covered from the same sources. The necessary unskilled labor was conscripted and paid low wages, while foreign technicians and skilled workers were attracted by high salaries. A market for the output of the factories was provided by the armed forces, by import substitution, by displacing some handicrafts.[12]

Now, to return to our question, why did industrialization take place in Egypt and fail to occur in the Ottoman Empire? Tentative answers may be suggested. In the first place, the Ottoman Empire of the nineteenth century did not have as bold an industrial program as that pursued by Muhammad Ali. Secondly, the Ottoman Empire lacked the leadership, understanding, and the desire to industrialize: characteristics all combined in the ruler of Egypt. Thirdly, internal resistance to Muhammad Ali's policies, whether organized or not, was weak. In the Ottoman Empire, internal opposition to any type of Western "product" was too strong. Fourthly, some of the Foreign Powers, particularly France, showed an interest in helping Egypt industrialize. France sought immediate political objectives, such as the further weakening of the influence of the Porte and of Britain in Egypt, so she could be free to deal with the autonomous state as she pleased. However, this experiment in industrializing a backward nation led to the strengthening of the belief of the Great Powers that the industrialization of underdeveloped countries should not be artificially fostered, especially in those countries that abounded in raw materials which could be of use to the industries of the Western nations.

Supposing, then, that the Ottoman Empire were to have embarked upon some type of industrialization other than railways—that is the construction of factories for the production of goods—what would have been the major institutional impediments standing in its way? Some of these obstacles are herein briefly discussed. They are neither presented in their order of importance nor are they exhaustive. Their discussion is intended to identify the kind of obstacles that would have to be overcome if industrialization were to have been achieved. It is worthy of note that the presence of the *millet* system, the capitulatory regime, the peculiar tariff system which had to be fixed by conventions, etc. gave the Ottoman Empire a unique set of problems to cope with.

To begin with, industrialization was considered a Western "product" and automatically objected to by the Muslim masses. However, it could have been imposed. But for industrialization to have taken place, an enlightened, tolerant, efficient, independent, and strong government, to say the least, would have been a prerequisite for carrying out an industrial program. The primary target of the government would have been the removal of the sources of conservatism which opposed change. This first step was achieved by Mahmud II, for by annihilating the Janissaries and starting a process of weakening the power of the Ulema, he softened the ground for himself and for his followers to pursue liberal reforms.

The second objective, that of assimilating the different *millets* within the empire so that immense national benefits could be reaped, was given only lip service by the *Hatti Sherif of Gulhane* and the *Hatti Humayun*. By giving the non-Muslim *millets* additional rights and privileges instead of progressing towards assimilation and fusion, even greater resentment was expressed by the Muslims, who interpreted these gestures as favoritism towards the non-Muslim minorities. The task of integration became still harder. Unfortunately, the destruction of the conservative powers, symbolized by the Ulema and the Janissaries and the new laws favoring the minorities, did not by themselves create new attitudes, new values, and liberal modes of thought. They were of valuable assistance and in the right direction. But the hatred of Western ideology by the masses continued to persist. In spite of their waning power, the Ulema continued to abet the anti-Western cause.

Other attempts at infusing new ideologies were tried through the educational system, which was expanded and removed from the hands of the Ulema. But ideologies which were necessary for industrialization could neither be developed overnight nor utilized by rulers who did not have a clear cut objective. Educating the masses, the bulk of whom were imbued with nationalistic and religious fervor, was a protracted project in any case, with no guarantee of reform on Western lines.

However, instead of proceeding with further reforms which could have led to the creation of a liberal and enlightened stratum in Ottoman society, the Sultans were interested in centralizing authority in their own hands. In pursuing this course they set aside the fundamental elements of their reform movement, and instead used these reforms as a pretext for getting accepted in the Concert of European nations and for borrowing capital on European markets, whether to meet the needs of the military, to defray their personal expenses, or to help in railway development.

Thirdly, the Ottoman Government was circumscribed by its lack of political and economic autonomy and could not pursue an independent course of action. There was need for internal security and a different attitude towards wars and insurrections. The shackles of the capitulations had to be removed. Turkey needed to act independently to change her tariffs, rather than be subjected to conventions and to the full agreement of all the Powers concerned. Many of the rights and privileges enjoyed by the foreigners and the non-Muslim *millets* had to be modified.

Fourthly, preparing the attitudes of the public to accept the ideologies of the West with regards to industrialization was only one major step. An extension of this step was necessary in the direction of the laboring class. The experience of underdeveloped economies in pursuing a course of industrial development points to the serious difficulties they have been experiencing in training labor in skills, infusing them with proper attitudes to work in industries, and helping them acquire and develop new habits and new values.

> But the overriding fact to consider is that industrial labor in the sense of a stable, reliable, and disciplined group that has cut the umbilical cord connecting it with the land has become suitable for utilization in factories is not abundant but extremely scarce in a backward country. Creation of an industrial labor force that really deserves its name is a most difficult and protracted process.[13]

Even to educate and train labor, one needs trainees, laborers who could stay on the job and not be called too often to serve the military: factories in which to train them, financially rewarding jobs with hope of continuity and progress, and a favorable political, social and economic "climate." All these and other enticements are necessary to lure the worker into an industrial project.

Fifthly, the development of a financial machinery to facilitate the flow of savings and capital into proper channels has to be accompanied by other improvements. Financial institutions, such as agricultural and industrial banking institutions, savings and loans associations, and insurance companies which pool capital resources and invest them properly, had to be organized and protected by laws. In the Ottoman Empire, there was need for capital, whether from local or foreign sources. True, large amounts of capital were raised in the European markets, part of which went into railway development; but most of it was expended on consumption goods and squandered unproductively. With the income of the empire mortgaged for decades to follow, difficulty in borrowing became common. Thus the shortage of capital continued to plague the Ottoman Empire until it finally plunged into the war of 1914.

Finally, one of the fields which was a prerequisite for industrial development was transportation, mainly in railways. Attention was also paid towards improving roads, ports, the telegraph system, etc. However, while Turkey was partially successful in helping to develop these, she failed to capitalize fully on these assets.

Therefore, in the absence of the necessary conditions for a profitable investment, capital had to look elsewhere. Capital by itself could not overcome institutional impediments.

To say that industrialization was costly and hence not a practical solution for an Ottoman Empire in heavy debt does not hold much water. If maintained by foreign enterprisers, industrialization need not have been costly to the Sultan, since it could have been pursued at no expense to the Government. But Governmental assistance was of the utmost importance. Among the basic conditions of a healthy investment climate should be included governmental aid in the form of laws and their implementation. Laws fostering industrialization, for example, such as the promulgation of laws favoring private ownership, free movement of capital and personnel, and general security, were essential in a country that was unfortunately better noted for its deficiencies in these respects. Furthermore, the Porte could have assigned a special security force to guard foreign investment. But this was not the intent or desire of the Sultan.

Although favorable conditions for investment were alluring in themselves and therefore the suggestions made above could have attracted more individual entrepreneurs, foreign investors in general, whether implicitly or explicitly supported by their governments, were not inclined to industrialize the Ottoman Empire. The industrial nations of the nineteenth century, though battling against one another, held tenaciously to a selfish but understandable argument. If agricultural nations were to specialize in the production of agricultural commodities and raw materials, thus assuring a continuous flow of factors at low prices on the one hand and goods on the other, then both parties stood to gain from this specialization through trade. The industrial nations were interested in insuring the full employment of their resources, which could eventually lead to prosperity and further development. The operation of their factories depended very much on the raw materials imported from the agricultural communities.

More specifically, the argument on specialization and hence the gain from trade rests on rigid Ricardian assumptions, which include free mobility of some of the factors and of commodities between regions and states.

It was also feared that were the Ottoman Empire to industrialize, at least two undesirable consequences with serious repercussions were thought likely to ensue: (a) by channeling their raw materials to local Ottoman industries, European nations would be deprived of these materials and could import them only at high prices. Besides, no nation was desirous of having a new competitor. In any event, this step could have led to unemployment and fluctuations in the economies of the European powers. It could have led to the removal of the capitulations, threatened British interests in India, and frustrated colonial plans by the Foreign Powers, as was revealed later.

(b) Secondly, no European nation seriously contemplated a Turkey whose power would jeopardize European interests within Turkey, or anywhere else. True, Great Britain at one time favored a stronger Turkey for the purpose of opposing Tzarist Russia and her designs for a window on the Black Sea, but the idea of supporting industrialization within Turkey was not entertained. The history of a powerful Eastern Empire that had knocked many times on the doors of Europe was still vivid in the minds of Europeans, and the whole concept of a powerful Ottoman Empire that could engage in successful offensive wars was unacceptable and rejected outright.

Finally, those designs of the Foreign Powers which aimed at dividing the "Sick Man of Europe" into zones of occupation precluded any kind of investment that might have strengthened Turkey in the long run and increased her resistance. These designs, finally revealed, found their fullest expression during World War I.

Because of their rivalries, the Foreign Powers might have frustrated any attempt at regional development by the Ottoman Empire. With respect to railways, it has been noted that each foreign government tried to influence the decisions of the Porte, the railway companies, and the financial markets where money was procured. Austria, France, Germany, Great Britain, Italy, and Russia were all concerned about their own interests in the Ottoman Empire, and interested in the impact that railway development might produce. Every Power wanted to know how railway development would affect its interests and those of others. Would it affect its trade relations, the status quo in the area, the integrity of the empire? Would it disturb the so-called imaginary spheres of influence, and would it have any influence on future designs? All these and other points of importance had to be weighed and evaluated by each Power separately. Since the motives and interests of the Great Powers were in conflict, each Power tried to act independently. That is why it is often said that Abdul Hamid capitalized on a situation in which he knew that the Foreign Powers were split against one another and thereby tried to get the best of the bargain whenever he dealt with one of them.

The question then arises as to whether gradual or regional industrialization was possible in the Ottoman Empire at all. The answer is affirmative. Had the Porte allowed its gradual undertaking, and provided the Foreign Powers consented, industrialization could have taken place. The fact is, however, that neither one of these two parties was interested.

In retrospect, the policies followed by Abdul Hamid in encouraging railway development to the exclusion of industrial development in other fields were in conformity with his character, with his wishes to maintain the integrity of the Ottoman Empire, and with the desires of the Foreign Powers. Therefore, to have attempted to persuade the Sultan to follow a different course might have been futile. To illustrate further, if one had asked him to enforce liberal reforms and carry out fundamental political and social changes which would have transformed the empire, the request would have fallen on deaf ears. The Sultan was bent on maintaining an autocratic and centralized regime. In a system of dictatorship there is room only for narrow and rigid policies. Flexibility is seldom permitted. Therefore, to have asked the Sultan to give autonomy or self-rule to distant provinces which were in reality a thorn in his flesh was akin to asking him to liquidate an empire that he was guarding, that had belonged to his ancestors. Besides, Turkey long cherished the hope of regaining lost territories. As Feis puts it:

> Turkey was arming to win back lost territory in Europe; when war came Turkey entered in a gamble to win lost strength and independence. The forces of the nineteenth century had pulled apart Turkish conquests of past centuries. The Ottoman Empire could not survive in its inherited form and boundaries within the world of newly strengthened nationalist European states. Foreign capital and modern industrial technique might have restored its power. They proved to be one of the forces which brought out all its inherent weakness. It requires an orderly and competent government and a healthy state to utilize them advantageously.[14]

It may be argued that Sultan Abdul Hamid, under whose reign most of the railway development took place, abhorred foreign intervention, and on these grounds he opposed industrialization. But this argument loses much of its strength once the reader is reminded that railways, which are one form of industrial development, were constructed, owned, and operated by foreigners.

E. *Conclusion*

The study of railway development in the Ottoman Empire presents a case of distorted development that has few parallels in the history of economic development. This uniqueness is not solely restricted to a mere set of facts that has been deduced about railway development *per se,* but more comprehensively, includes the institutional background and the concomitant changes that took place. To summarize, the railways in the Ottoman Empire were constructed, owned and operated principally by foreign companies. They were built over a long span of time and under severe hardships. They possessed different gauges and were principally one track lines. Many of them carried concessions which were guaranteed by the Porte and made good by the Public Debt Administration.

As to the economic consequences of railway development, it has been observed that they were largely confined to the agricultural sector of the economy and to related facilities in transportation. Since neither the mineral resources of the country were significantly exploited nor industrial development encouraged, only a limited impact was produced by railway development on the Turkish economy. Material benefits were thus confined and economic growth retarded. The expansion in agriculture and in foreign trade were necessary, but did not comprise sufficient conditions for economic development. The benefits of such a growth went to paying the Public Debt or were dissipated in greater consumption, leaving nothing for investment.

Finally, a continued development of the economic, political and social institutions was slow. The continued presence of the *millet* system in an autocratic regime bent on centralization did not foster smooth economic growth. In addition, the incessant wars that plagued the empire, the public debt, the low tariffs imposed by the Porte (whose abiilty to alter them was restricted by the Foreign Powers) all conspired to restrict the rate of economic development in Turkey. The emphasis on railways could not by itself bring about strong advances in the economy. It was not enough by itself to sustain an aggressive drive. Certainly railway development facilitated development in the Ottoman

Empire, but it was not an overall cure to the fundamental ills that had to be eradicated. The experiences of the West have conclusively indicated that railway development had to be supported by fundamental institutional changes, if it is to have the hoped for results. The balanced growth achieved by industrializing several diverse areas is vitally necessary to prosperity in an industrial age, in the new world.

NOTES

CHAPTER I

1. Unless specific reference is made to Modern Turkey, **i.e., post** World War I Turkey, the terms 'Turkey' and 'Ottoman Empire' are used interchangeably.
2. Gordon, James Leland, **American Relations with Turkey 1830-1930, An Economic Interpretation,** University of Pennsylvania Press, 1932, p. 130.
3. Lewis, Bernard, **The Emergence of Modern Turkey,** Oxford University Press, London, 1961, p. 36.
4. Morawitz, Charles, **Les Finances de la Turquie,** Paris, 1902, p. 14.
5. Toynbee, Arnold J. and Kirkwood, Kenneth P., **Turkey,** New York, Charles Scribner's Sons, 1927, p. 259. On the same page, the following is added:

   "In the Treaty itself, the most important clauses were those dealing with the new frontiers of Turkey; the redistribution of the Ottoman Public Debt; the abolition of the Capitulation System and the Millet System; and the protection of minorities and exchange of populations." For a detailed and lengthy list of the losses in territory sustained by the Ottoman Empire between 1774 and 1923 see (i) **The Process of Change in the Ottoman Empire,** by Wilbur W. White, The University of Chicago Press, Chicago, Illinois, 1937. (ii) **The Ottoman Empire and Its Successors 1801-1927,** by William Miller, Cambridge University Press, 1936, 4th edition. (iii) **A Guide to Turkish Area Study,** by John Kingsley Birge, American Council of Learned Societies, Washington, 1949. In this Guide a chronological list of these losses is available.
6. Gordon, op. cit., p. vii, (Preface).
7. **Turkey in Asia,** (Prothero, G. W., editor) referred to from now on by this title, is one of the handbooks prepared under the direction of the Historical Section of the British Foreign Office No. 58, 1920, p. 2; this booklet is 17 pages long and unlike the one entitled 'Turkey in Europe,' is primarily a historical treatment of Ottoman relationships with the Arabs.
8. **Turkey in Europe,** referred to by this title, is also one of the handbooks prepared under the direction of the Historical Section of the British Foreign Office, No. 16, 1920, footnote (1), p. 1. Edited by G. W. Prothero.

9. **Michelsen, Edward, The Ottoman Empire and Its Resources,** London, William Spooner, 379, Strand 1854, p. 139.

10. **Rostow, W. W., The Stages of Economic Growth, A Non-Communist Manifesto,** Cambridge, University Press, 1960, p. 4. He defines the traditional society as "one whose structure is developed within limited production functions, based on pre-Newtonian science and technology, and on pre-Newtonian attitudes towards the physical world. Newton is here used as a symbol for that watershed in history when men came widely to believe that the external world was subject to a few knowable laws, and was systematically capable of productive manipulation."

11. Ibid., p. 17.

12. A word of caution is in place about a number of things: (a) Some sources investigated for research, have used a capital letter for certain words, others did not. For example, the word 'Sultan' is also written or quoted in the middle of a sentence as 'sultan.' The same goes for a number of words such as empire, powers, millet, etc.; (b) Particularly important is the spelling of names of individuals, places, battles, treaties, firmans (edicts), etc. Though a glossary is provided at the end of the book, no change has been made of quoted words. For example, Beirut may be spelled 'Beyrouth' or 'Beyrut,' Basra may be quoted Bussora; (c) Thirdly, some names have been changed. For instance, Constantinople is used in the text rather than today's Istanbul, Smyrna instead of Izmir. Some of these changes are also recorded at the end of this book; (d) Variations on the same name are often used. For example, derivations from the word Moslem or Mohammedan have the same meaning. Mahometans, Mohammedans, Muslims, Moslems, Islamic people, all mean the same thing, that is, followers of the prophet Mohammed who profess the Islamic faith.

13. The terms Turkey and Ottoman Empire will be used interchangeably, unless reference is made to modern post World War I Turkey. The size and character of the Ottoman Empire in the period under consideration must also be examined and clarified, since the empire kept shrinking during the nineteenth and early part of the twentieth centuries until modern Turkey finally emerged.

14. Michelsen, op. cit., p. 138; Davison, Roderic, **Reform and Westernization in the Ottoman Empire: 1856-1876,** Cambridge, Massachusetts, 1942, p. 46.

15. See Section E under Wars, for territorial changes in the 19th and early 20th centuries. In 1914, Turkey in Europe had been largely reduced to about 11,000 square miles, with an estimated

population of 1,891,000 persons. Refer also to **Turkey in Europe**, op. cit., p. 1.

16. Urquhart, David, **Turkey and Its Resources**, London, Saunders & Otley, 1833, p. 216.
17. Bailey, Frank Edgar, **British Policy and the Turkish Reform Movement 1826-1853**, Harvard University Press, 1942, p. 95.
18. Ibid., p. 97.
19. Ibid., p. 98.
20. Ibid., p. 99.
21. Ibid., pp. 110-111.
22. Davison, op. cit., Appendix A, pp. 503-504, on Ottoman Population.
23. Michelsen, op. cit., p. 141; on pp. 146-48, Michelsen divides the Ottoman Empire into three large sectors: (a) European Turkey (Rumili), (b) Asiatic Turkey (Anadulu), and (c) African Turkey (Garb). He also gives a listing of all the eyalets (vilayets or provinces) under Ottoman jurisdiction. See Appendix on Sultans.
24. Ibid., p. 141. Michelsen later adds on p. 143, "The Privy Council consists of the Grand Vizier, the Sheikhul-Islam, and the Ministry, with and without portfolio. The latter are: the Ministers of the Marine, of War, of Finance, and of Commerce; also of the Chef d'Artillerie, the President of the Divan, the Council of the Grand Vizier, the Director of the Imperial Privy-Purse, the Director of the Charitables and pious institutions, the Postmaster-General, and finally, the Sultana mother."
25. Ibid., p. 145.
26. Blaisdell, Donald C., **European Financial Control in the Ottoman Empire**, New York, Columbia University Press, 1929, p. 10.
27. Davison, op. cit., p. 190. With respect to government, the vilayet was governed by a vali, the sanjak by a mutassarif, the Kaza by a Kaimakam. Appointments to these posts were directly made by the Porte. The Commune or Nahiye was governed by a Mukhtar who was elected by the people of the commune. For a detailed discussion of the provincial government of the vilayet system, 1864-67, see Davison, op. cit., ch. 6, pp. 180-214.
28. DuValay, op. cit., p. 46, gives the new number of vilayets at 26.
29. Michelsen, op. cit., p. 145 (footnote*). "Every Vali or Mutessarif is likewise the Muhassil of the Liva where he resides; he is the representative of the executive power, and stands in direct correspondence with all ministers. In Constantinople he has a **Kapu Kiajassi** (representative). The Kaimakam of a Liva stands under the Vali or Mutessarif; the Muhassil corresponds directly with the minister of interior. In every Liva there is a sort of

municipality (medjlis), presided over by the Governor of the Liva, and the members of which are: Mal Mudir (excise collector), the Greek and Armenian Patriarch, Rabbi, Chodja Bashah (delegate of Christian municipality), and the Vudshuh (primate), who is elected by the inhabitants. A Mudir (steward) is at the head of every kaza; a Muchtar or Chodja Bashah of every Nahye, and a Kyaya of every village. The metropolis, Constantinople, belongs to none of the eyalets, but has a civic administration of its own."

30. Lewis, **op. cit.**, p. 174.
31. Birge, **op. cit.** Attention is also drawn to several books where wars and insurrections are listed. Among these books figure prominently: White, **op. cit.**; Toynbee and Kirkwood, **op. cit.** esp. Chronology, Appendix pp. 320-321; also, Miller, **op. cit.**
32. White, **op. cit.**, p. 6. "It is significant that the first appearance of the Ottomans in Asia Minor was marked by combat. The beginnings, the growth, and the subsequent decline of their empire were signalized by battle. War was the fundamental means by which territory was gained; similarly, war was also the primary method by which territory was lost. Throughout the six odd centuries that the Ottoman Empire existed, its fortunes were largely measured by the success in battle; and it has been only in the most recent times that there has been any great exception to the general rule that gain or loss in territory or prestige of the state has been by war."
33. Bailey, **op. cit.**, p. 137. "Turkey had been left bankrupt by the Russian war, which came at a time when she was just beginning to show life. Her finances were disrupted; the army which Mahmoud had created following the destruction of the Janissaries needed reorganization. For these reasons the Sultan's authority was not respected in the provinces."
34. Hoskins, Halford Lancaster, **British Routes to India**, Longmans, Green and Company, N.Y., 1928, p. 140. "Late in the month of May (1830), the expeditionary squadron sailed from Toulon for Algiers. There the fortifications were bombarded and destroyed with no great difficulty. The disembarkation of troops began on June 14, and by the first week in July the city of Algiers was taken together with the treasure of the ruling house, some forty million francs. The Bey thereupon capitulated completely, and signed a Convention giving up the control of all fortified coast cities in return for French protection and guarantee of freedom of religion. By the end of July, 30,000 French soldiers were encamped along the Algerian sea-board."
35. Bailey, **op. cit.**, footnote (10), p. 5. "It might be said that Algeria, Tunis, and Tripoli were to all intents and purposes free at the

beginning of the nineteenth century; they completely disregarded the Sultan, their Suzerain, and since he had no powerful fleet it was almost impossible to subject them to this law."

36. For a detailed and more comprehensive study of reforms and other institutional developments, consult one of the most recent books, **The Emergence of Modern Turkey** by Bernard Lewis, Oxford University Press, London, 1961.

    On June 17, 1826, an imperial firman (edict) was issued. It declared the Corps of the Janissaries abolished, and its members outlaws. The word 'Janissary' is derived from Turkish 'yeni cheri' meaning new soldiers. It was the name given to a special corps that guarded the Sultan. Its members were recruited from Christian youth provided in partial payment of tribute by the Balkan States. This process was started in the 14th and continued until the 19th century. The recruits were subjected to intensive training, education and eventual screening for administrative and military positions. For a terse study on the development and activities of the Janissaries, see Bailey, **op. cit.**, pp. 23-38; the **Encyclopedia of Islam**, "The Janissaries," Toynbee & Kirkwood, **op. cit.**, p. 23.

37. Mardin, Serif, **The Genesis of Young Ottoman Thought**, Princeton University Press, 1962, p. 18, footnote (17), " 'Ulema' is the name used for the members of the Ilmyye, the 'order' which was made up of doctors of Islamic law and also included teachers and the personnel officiating mosques."

38. Bailey, **op. cit.**, p. 33.

39. Mardin, **op. cit.**, p. 133.

40. The Young Ottomans were a handful of patriotic reformers in Turkey. They sought to arrest the process of Ottoman decline. They stirred the public with their pen, particularly in the third quarter of the 19th century, and tried unsuccessfully to overthrow the government. After the abrogation of the constitution by Abdul Hamid in 1877, their activities were suppressed.

41. Lewis, Bernard, **The Emergence of Modern Turkey**, Oxford Press, 1961, p. 96.

42. See Section on Wars.

43. Bailey, **op. cit.**, pp. 136-137. "Following the signing of the treaty of Adrianople (1829) which concluded the Russo-Turk War and established the independence of Greece, Mahmoud again took up the cause of reform. He abolished feudal officials in the provinces. He established the beginnings of a modern cabinet in which officials could be held more responsible for their particular tasks. He took steps to overcome bribery. A passport system was established. Lighthouses were built at certain dangerous points

on the coast to protect shipping. Improved methods of controlling cholera and other diseases were established by the inauguration of a more rigid quarantine."

44. The Treaty of Unkier Skelessi, of July 8, 1833, concluded between Turkey and Russia, included a secret article which permitted Russian troops to come to the aid of Turkey in case of attack, and in case of war Turkey was to close the Dardanelles to the war-ships of all nations.

45. Bailey, **op. cit.**, p. 61.

46. Webster, Sir Charles Kingsley, **The Foreign Policy of Palmerston, 1830-1841**, vol. I, p. 76.

47. Toynbee & Kirkwood, **op. cit.**, p. 27, footnote (6). " 'Millets'—an Arabic word for which there is no equivalent in Western political terminology because it expresses an incommensurable order of political ideas."

    In the latter part of the 19th century, **millet** has been used synonymously with nation.

    As used by the above authors, 'millet' will be written with a small 'm.' For details on the **millet** system, see the Social Structure.

48. Bailey, **op. cit.**, p. 228. "The reforms of these years, (1823-1853) though not far reaching in themselves, did pave the way for the more extensive reforms of a later period."

49. Gulhane, literally means a rose-house, a chamber. For a complete translation and presentation of the **Hatti Sherif of Gulhane,** see Bailey, **op. cit.**, Appendix IV, pp. 277-279.

    Also, Bailey remarks, footnote (81), p. 146, "Financial difficulties, brought on by an ancient fiscal evil, such as 'avania' (extortions by the pashas) was one of the causes for the promulgation to the Hatti Sherif de Gulhane in 1839. A stronger government was necessary to overcome the critical financial situation faced by the Sultan in 1839."

50. Commenting on points of simiarity and difference between the two edicts, Davison, **op. cit.**, p. 31, states: "Both were cast in the most solemn form of imperial decree. Their texts were somewhat alike, though the later edict was an extension of the earlier. Both were promulgated when the Ottoman Empire was deeply involved in international complications. Both were aimed in large measure at satisfying European opinion. But the Hatti-Humayun was an autochthonous act in form alone; in reality it was simple dictation to the Turkish government by England, France, and Austria."

51. Bailey, **op. cit.**, Appendix IV, p. 277.

52. Mardin, **op. cit.**, p. 156.

53. Mardin, **op. cit.,** p. 157.
54. Bailey, **op. cit.,** Appendix VI, p. 287. The complete Hatt is available in Appendix VI, pp. 287-292.
55. Bailey, **op. cit.,** p. 290. On the same page, footnote (1) the following is added: "On Jan. 18, 1867, a law was passed granting to foreigners the right to hold real property in the Ottoman Empire; and on July 28, 1868, a protocol was signed between the British and Turkish governments relative to the admission of British subjects to the right of holding real property in Turkey."
56. Further discussion on reforms will be taken up when deemed necessary in the relevant sections.
57. Mardin, **op. cit.,** p. 18.
58. Emin, **op. cit.,** p. 14.
59. Waugh, Sir Telford, **Turkey, Yesterday, Today and Tomorrow,** Chapman's and Hall, London, 1930, p. 18.
60. Prothero, **Turkey in Europe,** op. cit., p. 34.
61. Toynbee & Kirkwood, op. cit., p. 48 "His (Midhat's) constitution was set aside by Abul'l- Hamid and replaced by an obscurantist and murderous personal government, of one of the earliest victims of Midhat himself."

BOOK I

CHAPTER II

1. **Lewis, op. cit., p. 259.**
2. Karal, Enver Ziya, "Historiography in Turkey Today," **Middle Eastern Affairs, Oct. 1959, Vol. X, No. 10, p. 318. "Up to World War I there were three concepts of history in Turkey—religious, dynastic and national. The most common was the religious; it symbolized the glorious history of Islam and aimed at maintaining the integrity of the Muslim World. The claim that the war had a holy character was based on this concept."**
3. **See previous section on Reforms for more information on the Ulema.**
4. **This classification is adopted by Bailey, op. cit., pp. 8-9. In footnote (17) p. 9. "Approximately three and a half million or about one-tenth of the total population were of this official class according to** Marshal Marmont, **The Present State of Turkey, London, 1839, p. 95.**
5. **Ibid.,** footnote (18), p. 9. **"Marmont suggests that this element in the population made reform difficult both because they were regarded by many old Turks as potential enemies of the state, and also because they opposed a regenerated Turkey which might further limit their power."**
6. **Ibid., pp. 9-10. "The remainder of the population constituted the third group; here are found the poorer classes, chiefly peasants and artisans, those who bore the brunt of the burdens, the majority of whom were Christians."**
7. Mears, **op. cit., p. 113.**
8. **Toynbee & Kirkwood, op. cit., p. 142. "The system was originally intended to simplify the task of government for the Sublime Porte and to relieve it from the embarrassment of administering the local affairs of the alien communities under Ottoman hegemony. Also, it was almost a necessary arrangement, in view of the fact that the law of the Quran which was civil as well as religious. could not be applied integrally to Christian communities."**
9. Toynbee and Kirkwood, **op. cit., p. 142.**
10. **Michelsen, op. cit.,** p. 140.
11. **Toynbee & Kirkwood, op. cit., p. 28.**
12. **Ibid.,** p. 28.
13. Prothero, **Turkey in Europe, p. 104.**
14. **Prothero, Turkey in Eruope, op. cit., p. 6.**

15. Mears, Elliot Grinnell, **Modern Turkey**, New York, Macmillan Co., 1924, p. 79, Chapter III, in Mears deals with the "Leading Minorities: their achievements and aspirations." It is divided into three articles. Mears admits in his introduction that some legitimate propaganda pervaded these articles which are: (i) "Armenians," by Boghos Nubar Pasha, pp. 63-75, (ii) "The Greeks," by Adamantios Th. Polyzoides, pp. 76-85, and (iii) "Jews," by His Eminence, Haim Nahoum, pp. 89-94.

15. Mears, **op. cit.**, p. 113.

16. Davison, **op. cit.**, p. 149. Of lesser importance were the Roman Armenians, Jewish, Roman Catholic and Protestant **millets.** No figures are given on their numbers. Michelsen, **op. cit.**, p. 140, gives the following estimates: The Greeks and Armenians: 13,730,000; Roman Catholics: 900,000; Jews: 170,000. On p. 141, Michelsen mentions the presence of 2,000 Protestants. It must be remembered that these figures were estimates of the 1850's. In the absence of proper censuses, or even a census at all, estimates vary widely. Disagreement on population figures is not uncommon.

17. Mears, **op. cit.**, p. 361.

18. Fraser, David, **The Short Cut to India**, William Blackwood & Sons, London, 1909, p. 19. "In the year 1864 a Greek engineer named Trypani imported a small machine for cotton-ginning. This was the first effort of modern enterprise in Cilicia, and, incidentally, the beginning of the fortunes of the firm of Trypani Brothers, which now has established at Adana factories and machinery at work, and in course of erection, in Cilicia, comprised the following:

Tarsus	Ginning-Machines	150
	Spindles	6,000
	Spindles (being erected)	20,000
	Weaving-looms (being erected)	400
Adana	Ginning-Machines	300
	Spindles	12,000
	Looms	200
	Flour-mills	10
District	Threshing-machines	60
	Steam-ploughs	4
	Reaping-machines	1,000
	Pumps, large and small	200
	Steam & Gas-engines	50

All of the above machinery is British, with the exception of the reaping machines, which are American. But for one small German concern, which is only the beginning of a much larger project, the industrial machinery is owned and worked by Greeks, and the agricultural machines by Turks. One or two of the engines are German gas-engines, but the great bulk are old-fashioned steam-engines, built on the Clyde or in the Midlands. Most of this machinery has been imported by the Trypani firm for their own account, or for others, and the total import may be said to be due to their intiation. Thus, though there is not a born Briton at Adana or Tarsus, our reputation for the manufacture of machinery seems to have remained undiminished."

19. Mears, op. cit., p. 67.
20. Mears, op. cit., p. 67. It is essential to bear in mind what Mears had warned in his book which is primarily a collection of articles, that some exaggerations were unavoidable. The Armenians 'controlled nearly all the domestic commerce' is certainly open to question. How near is nearly?
21. Michelsen, op. cit., p. 140.
22. Mears, op. cit., p. 87.
23. Mears, op. cit., p. 94.
24. Davison, op. cit., p. 53. "The effendis known also as Kiatibs and collectively as the Kalemiya, were the bureaucrats of the Porte and its provincial administrations. All three terms referred to the ability of these officials to read and write, which accomplishments were considered the mark of the educated men."
25. Bailey, op. cit., p. 78. "The most cursory study of Turkish commerce proves that the Turks as a people were not a nation of traders. That as individuals they drove shrewd bargains no traveller in Turkey would dispute, but collectively, when compared with some of the Western states, they appear most un-commercial. The fact was that the majority of merchants and bankers in Turkey were not Turks."

    Of course, they never had a formal or informal training in business activities and many lacked interest.
26. In describing the economic problems facing the New Republic of Turkey after World War I, Toynbee and Kirkwood lament the absence of the dynamic element of the minorities in commerce, trade and industry. In its desire for reconstruction, they state: op. cit., p. 226, "Angora was faced with the gigantic problem created by the removal of almost all the Greek, Armenian and other non-Turkish minorities which had woven the warp of commerce in the woof of Turkish agriculture in the economic fabric

of the Old Ottoman Empire. The principal elements of the country were gone."

In fact, a large vacuum was created after World War I in Turkey. The inexperienced Turks had to take over the business activity which was handled for many generations by the well experienced and seasoned Greeks and Armenians.

27. Bailey, op. cit., p. 141, also taken from Marmont, Marshal (Duc de Raguse) **The Present State of the Turkish Empire**, translated with notes and observations by Lt. Col. Sir Frederick Smith, London, 1839, p. 324. Waugh, op. cit. states: " 'Dans l'armée turque,' wrote in 1854 the French Maréchal de Saint Arnaud, 'il y a deux choses, un général en chef et des soldats. De point intermédiaire aucun. Il n'a pas d'officiers et encore moins de sous officiers.' "

28. Blaisdell, op. cit., p. 75. "Potential resources existed within her borders, but Turkey lacked the technical skill and capital for their development. The limited amounts of native capital were in the hands of the subject races, Greeks, Armenians, Jews. It is doubtful whether sufficiently large sums could have been realized from this source to develop Turkish natural resources effectively."

True as this may be, had the non-Muslim millets pooled their resources and started developing, gradual exploitation of the natural resources and industrialization could have snowballed giving rise to profits and inviting foreign investors to help by all means. However, this is mere speculation.

29. Blaisdell, op. cit., p. 39, who also refers to Charles Morawitz, **Les Finances de la Turquie**, Paris, 1902, "Bankers in Galata (the section of Constantinople containing the financial district) who had engaged in lending to the Government, retired to Paris and constructed mansions in the Parc Monceau."

30. Davison, op. cit., pp. 403-404.

31. Bailey, op. cit., p. 211, footnote (9) (taken from Edmund Spencer, **Travels in European Turkey**, London, 1851, Vol. I, p. 269). "In a country where the unlettered son of a cobbler is eligible to the office of a Pacha or Vizier, according to the caprice of the sovereign, or the influence of bribery; a change in the authorities only adds to the evil, by substituting a poor man for a rich one, who must have recourse to extortion to support his new dignity. . . . This state of things cannot endure, an aristocracy of hungry officials, is one of the greatest curses that can be inflicted upon a country, and most assuredly has principally contributed to the decadence of the Turkish Empire."

32. Emin, Ahmed, **The Development of Modern Turkey as Measured by its Press**, Columbia Press, N.Y. 1914, p. 11.

CHAPTER III

1. Toynbee & Kirkwood, op. cit., p. 212.
2. Ibid., p. 218, "The Turkish farmer has shown apathy because of the uncertainty caused by the wandering bands of brigands who were liable at any moment to descend upon a village and rob it of its wealth."
3. Gordon, op. cit,. p. 72. "In the past the fact that agriculture formed the basis of its economic life was the source of its greatest strength, enabling it to survive in spite of an inefficient government and many years of continuous warfare."
4. Toynbee & Kirkwood, op. cit., p. 212. "The methods of cultivation which they (the Turks) employ resemble those in use at the dawn of history. A crooked stick tipped with flint and drawn by water-buffalo or oxen is the accepted plough. Deep ploughing, the use of fertilizers, and the advantages of crop rotation are still unknown. Modern machinery for sowing and reaping is merely an object of curiosity; both tasks are done by hand. There are threshing floors in all the villages, where the grain, brought in by the peasants, is threshed by dragging over it heavy logs of wood studded with flint. The process of winnowing is usually performed by tossing the grain into the air. In the absence of mills, it is a common sight throughout Anatolia to see grain being crushed between stones, and the old disused millstones lie by many a forsaken road where a farm house now deserted, or ruined by fire, once stood."
5. Fraser, op. cit., p. 77; see also the section on Social Structure.
6. See Tables in Prothero, G.W., Turkey in Europe, pp. 120-126.
7. Bailey, op. cit., p. 93. "The one raw material of which Turkey had virtual monopoly as far as Britain was concerned was valonia, a by-product of acorns, which was used by tanners in the English leather industry." The period covered is 1823-1853.
8. Ibid., p. 85. Commenting on trade between 1823 and 1853, Bailey pp. 90-91 remarks: "While Turkey's exports to the United Kingdom were primarily soil-products, they included not only foodstuffs and luxury articles but raw materials for the manufacturers as well. One of the most important in this last category was madder root, used in the dying of textiles."
9. Prothero, Turkey in Europe, op. cit., pp. 92-93. Foreigners, at their own risk, held property through a Muslim dummy representative.

10. Davison, op. cit., p. 315.
11. Mears, op. cit., p. 371.
12. Ibid., p. 371. Though the treatment of mines is general, it furnishes a clue to the limited mining activities in a very wealthy mining community.
13. Urquhart, op. cit., p. 371. "The copper mines of Gune, whose produce receives the designation of Tocat, Trebizone, and Diarbekir, from the places where it is wrought, or where it receives a second smelting, and whence it is exported to Persia, to India, or shipped for Constantinople, the shores of the Black Sea, and etc., is perhaps the richest copper mine in the world; the hills seem one mess of carbonate of copper."
14. Gordon, op. cit., p. 80.
15. DuValay, A., Histoire Financière de la Turquie, Paris, 1902, p. 621.
16. Gordon, op. cit., p. 80.
17. See Prothero, Turkey in Europe, op. cit., pp. 102-103. Further information on industry will be given later in the following chapters.
18. Gordon, op. cit., p. 73. "One reason Turkey is so backward in manufacturing industries is because the European Concert of Powers which so long controlled the customs duties of that country refused to permit the imposition of rates high enough to encourage the building up of factories in Turkey. The 11 per cent 'ad valorem' rate which prevailed so many years was a tariff for revenue only."

    As a passing comment on industrialization, electricity was scarcely used in Turkey during the reign of Abdul Hamid, who, it is said, thought that dynamo and dynamite were identical.
19. See Annex B for the entire estimate of the budget by Michelsen, whose estimate, though not wholly exact, gives an idea of Turkey's expenditures and revenues for that period. Refer to Michelsen, op. cit., p. 173.
20. One pound sterling roughly equals one Turkish pound, ten kurush. (It equals 1 T.L. 10 kurush; T.L. is the abbreviation for Turkish Livre or Turkish Lira).

    Note that Morawitz, op. cit., p. 20, estimates Turkey's receipts prior to the Crimean War at T.L. 7,510,000 only 200,000 more than Michelsen. In fact, the land taxes were estimated at 2,200,000 rather than at T.L. 2,000,000.
21. Blaisdell, op. cit., p. 36.
22. £1 equals 25 Frs. equals T.L. 1:10.
23. For a detailed estimate, see DuValay, op. cit., p. 176.
24. Morawitz, op. cit., p. 14.

25. Morawitz, op. cit., p. 20. "There are certain things that one learns very rapidly. The art of getting in debt falls in this category; hardly initiated, Turkey began making long strides."
26. Ibid., p. 14.
27. Bailey, op. cit., p. 159.
28. Waugh, op. cit., p. 15.
29. Blaisdell, op. cit., p. 27. Blaisdell also adds to this: "On Aug. 4, 1854, Sultan Abdul Medjid issued a firman (edict) authorizing a loan of three million pounds sterling. The contract was awarded to Dent, Palmer, and Company, of London, and their Paris agents, Goldsmidt and Company. The interest rate was six percent, with one percent annual amortization, and the issue price was eighty.

    Underwriters' commissions and the low issue price decreased the receipts from this loan to half of the nominal amount. The sum realized by the Ottoman Treasury was inadequate to meet the demands of the war."
30. Correa, H.M.A., The International Controls of Public Finance, Krukkering M. H. Portielzie, Amsterdam, 1926, p. 64. Of particular interest in this field are the works by Correa, DuValay, Morawitz and Blaisdell, op. cit., several loans were arranged by European Financiers in European markets, especially in London and Paris. Bonds were issued and loans were secured to the Sultan in large amounts that carried heavy interest and amortization rates. Correa, op. cit., p. 64, further reveals that "In 1875 the expenses for the debt service (318 million Francs) were nearly just as high as the total revenue of Turkey."
31. Moharrem denotes the Turkish month in which final agreement was reached. The Decree of Moharrem was later supplemented by another decree. See Blaisdell, op. cit., pp. 90-92; on page 97 he states: "The Decret-Annexe, or Supplementary Decree of Sept. 14, 1903, accomplished two definite objects: the unification of the unredeemed bonds, replacing them by a new issue; and the abolition of those articles of the earlier decree concerning the ability of the Government to participate in profits."
32. Mears, op. cit., p. 400. See particularly Chapter XVII, "The Public Treasury," by William Wilson Cumberland, pp. 384-410.
33. Toynbee & Kirkwood, op. cit., p. 234.
34. Blaisdell, op. cit., p. 30. "This extravagance prompted the following caustic comment from a Constantinople banker: It is monstrous that the finances of a great empire should be ruined by the fantastic desires of a fool who, already having fifty palaces, wants to construct fifty more."
35. Toynbee & Kirkwood, op. cit., p. 136. "Capitulations were 'capi-

tula' or 'articles' voluntarily granted in accordance with established tradition by the early Ottoman Government to foreign communities resident in its territories."

For further reference on capitulations, consult (i) **The Encyclopedia of Social Science**, pp. 213-214, "Capitulations," by Phillip Marshall Brown. (ii) Mears, **op. cit.**, Chapter 19, pp. 430-447, "Capitulations," by G. B. Ravndall. (iii) Toynbee & Kirkwood, **op. cit.**, pp. 136-140.

36. Mears, **op. cit.**, p. 437. "Even as the Moslem law was not made for the foreigner because he was a non-Moslem, the law can neither protect him, nor judge him, nor punish him. The foreigner must, therefore, be protected, judged and punished by his own law."

37. For details on tariffs, consult Bailey, **op. cit.**, pp. 120-125; Gordon, **op. cit.**, pp. 160-177; and Chapman, Maybelle Rebecca, **Great Britain and the Bagdad Railway 1888-1914.** Northampton, Massachusetts, 1948.

In order to curry favor with European Powers, Sultans since Suleiman the Magnificent, allowed imports a low tariff duty. This stems from two basic points: (i) that the Ottoman Empire respected free trade and offered hospitality and protection to foreign traders regardless of nationality, hence it continued to respect the capitulatory regime; (ii) revenue was not considered a factor in tariff considerations.

38. Bailey, **op. cit.**, p. 125.

39. **Encyclopedia of Social Sciences**, p. 213. "In the treaty of Adrianople in 1454, Turkey and Venice specified a duty of 2% on goods sold by Venetian Merchants in Turkish ports. It was also stipulated that Turkey could not change this tariff when signing with other powers having capitulatory rights."

40. Bailey, **op. cit.**, p. 78. "Why the Turkish Government reversed the usual action of tariffs has never been fully explained. Even the need for more money to manage their ever-growing governmental administration was not enough to induce them to change their traditional tariff policy. Instead of introducing a tariff for revenue purposes only the government preferred to increase taxes or depreciate the currency. When these methods were not sufficient, rather than borrow, the Sultan debased the coinage still further, thereby subjecting the people to double taxation."

Note that in the middle of the 19th century, the importance of tariffs for revenue was recognized. Perhaps, increased expenditures by the Sultans forced this recognition. Unfortunately, this recognition could not be enforced because of the capitulation system.

41. According to Chapman, Britain had opposed any tariff raise on the part of Turkey between 1890 and 1907, lest the revenues from the increase should go towards guaranteeing the construction of railways, particularly the Berlin-Bagdad Railway by the Germans, to which she was opposed.

Gordon, op. cit., p. 161, remarks: "Up to August 6, 1929, the Government of Turkey was deprived of complete sovereignty in its customs legislation, although it claimed and exercised sovereignty after its entrance into the war in 1914 and in spite of the protests of European powers. Through the privileges and powers extended by the capitulations and subsequent special treaties negotiated by the Sultans with various European governments, the right of the Ottoman Government to raise its customs duties was subject to the approval of each of the powers. As a result the customs duties on merchandise entering Turkey were kept at a nominal rate so that the maunfacturers of England, France, Germany and the other powers might enjoy an unrestricted market in Turkey.

11. According to Chapman, Britain had opposed any tariff raise on the part of Turkey between 1890 and 1907, but the revenues from the increase would go towards guaranteeing the construction of railways, particularly the Berlin-Baghdad railway by the Germans, to which she was opposed.

Dietrich, op. cit., p. 161, remarks: "Up to August 6, 1924, the Government of Turkey was deprived of complete sovereignty in its customs legislation, although it claimed and exercised nominal [illegible] protests of European powers. Through the privileges and powers extended by the capitulations and subsequent special treaties negotiated between Sultans with various European governments, the right of the Ottoman Government to raise its customs duties was subject to the approval of the powers. As a result the customs duties on merchandise entering Turkey were kept at a nominal rate so that the manufacturers of England, France, Germany and other powers might enjoy an unrestricted market in Turkey."

BOOK II

CHAPTER I

1. Prothero, Turkey in Europe, op. cit., p. 62. "The Straits of the Bosphorus, commonly called the Bosphorus, divided the vilayet of Constantinople into two parts. The European side is generally spoken of in Turkish as the Rumelian side, and the Asiatic side as the Anatolian. The length of the Straits is about 16 nautical miles. At the Marmora entrance the width is about 3,200 yards. The narrowest point is between Rumelli-Hissar and Anatoli-Hissar, where the width is only 1200 yards. The average depth of the Bosphorus is over 30 fathoms, the greatest depth (53 fathoms) being found in its narrowest parts." (1 fathom equals 6 feet; 1,000 fathoms equal 1 nautical mile).
2. Davison, op. cit., p. 100.
   Michelsen, op. cit., p. 186, makes these remarks (around the 1850's) "Turkey possesses, as yet, no roads; the few which were made in the ante-Osmanic reigns, having long since fallen into decay and become impassable. The farmers, consequently, can transport and bring their productions to market only in the vicinity of the coast; while, in the interior, their sales are confined to the consumption of the provincial towns, the inhabitants of which being themselves mostly employed in agriculture. The means of transporting goods from and to the coast are confined to camel and mule, a mode of conveyance which is so expensive that only the more valuable goods can bear the cost. Hence it happens, that the farmer limits his crops to his own wants and consumption."
3. Gordon, op. cit., p. 75, Mears, op. cit., p. 217. "Owing to the inclination of the Plateau to the northwest, over half the rivers flow into the Black Sea and the Sea of Marmara. They follow a tortuous course and yet are short compared to the rivers of other countries. The Kizil Irmak, one of the largest of Anatolian rivers, is about 550 miles in length but if it were straight it would be no more than 125 miles long. Because of their steep upper courses the rivers are not well adapted to usage for irrigation and for the same reason they frequently overdrain their basins."
4. Fraser, op. cit., p. 74.

5. Gordon, **op. cit.**, p. 78.
6. Urquhart, **op. cit.**, p. 133. "It is thus that, notwithstanding the commerce of the East, without exchanges of post offices, canals or railroads, insurances or credit; unprotected by courts at home, or consuls abroad; unprotected by a legislative body, where all interests are duly represented, extends its gigantic operations from Mount Atlas to the Yellow Sea; from the Blue mountains amid the deserts of Africa, to the Baikal in the wastes of Tartary and by the slow and noiseless step of the camel maintains the communications, exchanges the produce, and supplies the wants of three-fourths of the globe."
7. Fraser, **op. cit.**, p. 71. "Stately camels sailed noiselessly along in endless strings; bunches of tiny donkeys pattered by, care in their steps and deep wisdom upon their thoughtful brows, silly pack-horses neighed loudly as they recognized their own kind toiling up the hill-side."

   This is indeed an amusing and interesting comment by a Scot. It puts in a nutshell valuable information on how commodities were transported in those days.
8. Michelsen aptly sums up the economic situation in the Ottoman Empire on the eve of the Crimean War. If only heed had been taken. Michelsen, **op. cit.**, pp. 184-188. "The enumeration of the causes which still operate so injuriously on agriculture, constitutes almost the only statistical information we are enabled to furnish on this important branch." Then he goes on to elaborate every one of the following causes: 1. the general indolence of the country people; 2. want of laborers, 3. want of capital, 4. wants of means of communication."
9. The Imperial Firman is available in full in Hoskins, **op. cit.**, p. 161, see also p. 426. Commercial navigation on the Tigris and Euphrates rivers has an interesting history which is discussed at length by Hoskins. Of particular interest in the second quarter of the 19th century was the British desire to open a shorter, perennially navigable and more usable route—a 'short-cut,' to link the Mediterranean with India, rather than depend on the one through Egypt and the Red Sea. For another exciting account, see Fraser, **op. cit.**, pp. 264-272.
10. Hoskins, **op. cit.**, p. 428.
11. It must be remembered that among the limitations confronting the Lynch Brothers, were (a) the regulations imposed that their firm could not use more than two steam boats at a time regardless of traffic; (b) that dues had to be paid and palms of so many officials in Constantinople and Bagdad had to be greased; (c)

that the Tigris river was confined to vessels only twenty to fifty tons burden, etc. However, these limitations were not too serious considering the profits realized and the services rendered. The Lynch steamers were of essential service, providing convenient, dependable and a speedy method of transmitting packets between the Persian Gulf and points on the coast of Syria.

CHAPTER II

1. Feis, Herbert, Europe the World's Banker, 1870-1914, Preface, p. XV "When in the stillness of some distant, uninhabited valley the steam shovels and pneumatic drills pound out the path for steel rails and the locomotive, a drama of new life is begun. Human power is applying itself to an intricate creation. One world is destroyed, another founded."
2. For more detailed studies on railway development in the Ottoman Empire, refer to the following list which is by no means exhaustive: Chapman, op. cit., pp. 17-42; DuValay, op. cit., pp. 245-260 and 547-633; Earle, E. M., Turkey, the Great Powers, and the Bagdad Railway, Chapters 1-3; Feis, op. cit., Chapters 13 & 15; Fraser, op. cit.,; Gordon, op cit., Chapter 8; Hoskins, op. cit., pp. 222-231; Jastrow, M., The War and the Bagdad Railway, Chapter 3; Mears, op. cit., Chapter 9; British Handbooks: Anatolia, Mesopotamia, Turkey in Asia and Turkey in Europe; Nos. 59, 63, 58 and 15 respectively.

   Also the following articles: Dominian, Leon, "Railroads in Turkey," Bulletin of the American Geographical Society, XLVII, (1915) pp. 934-44; Newcombe, S. F. and Greig, J. P. S. "The Bagdad Railway," Geographical Journal, 44, (1914) pp. 577-80; Stewart, Charles and Hoss, Salim, Railroads, Politics and Regional Development in the Fertile Crescent" Al Ab'hath, Dec. 1961; Woods, H. Charles, "The Bagdad Railway and its Tributaries," Geographical Journal, L, (1917), pp. 32-56.
3. Hoskins, op. cit., p. 328.
4. 1 kilometre equals 0.621 mile.
5. Originally, the concession of 1856 carried with it a provision that the Turkish Government should pay a 6% annual interest on the original capital. For one reason or another, the provision was put in abeyance.
6. Chapman, op. cit., p. 17, erroneously states that the Smyrna-Aidin line was opened in 1877. Also (L.D.) Bulletin of the American Geographical Society, loc. cit., 1915, p. 935, errs in saying that "Its (the Smyrna Aidin line) construction began in 1856."
7. Though Baron Hirsch was a German, French and Austrian capital played a dominant role in the construction and operation of the Anatolian network. It was later controlled by the Deutsche Bank. Accordingly, investment in the Anatolian network could as

well be discussed in the section entitled: German Investment.

8. Mears, **op. cit.**, p. 224. "The Oriental Railway is poorly laid out, with no attempt at avoiding severe curves since an underlying plan in the construction was to obtain as large a mileage as possible in order to benefit from the kilometric guarantee. Thus, although Constantinople is only 148 miles distant from Adrianople, by highway, the railway was a length of 198 miles including 24 miles in Bulgarian territory."
9. Wood, **Geographical Journal**, April 1916, **loc. cit.**, p. 273. "By far the most important railway in the Balkan Peninsula is that which connects Belgrade with Constantinople. It constitutes the Balkan section of the great trunk route from West to East. Of its total length of 569 miles, 212 miles are in Serbia, 271 are in Bulgaria, and the remaining 176 miles are still in the Ottoman Empire."
10. Prothero, **Turkey in Europe, op. cit.**, p. 64. "The controlling interest in the Oriental Railway is in the hands of Austrians and Germans. The bulk of the share capital is held by the Banque des Chemins de fer Orientaux, a Swiss company formed in Zürich by the Deutsche Bank, the Schweizeriche Kreditanstalt, and the Wiener Bankverein for the purpose, amongst others, of taking over the 88,000 shares of the company belonging to the late Baron Hirsch."
11. The Balkan Wars had caused various adjustments in railway ownership, operation, etc. Refer to Feis, **op. cit.**, pp. 298-312. 298-312.
12. Woods, **Geographical Journal**, April 1916, **loc. cit.**, pp. 273-274.
13. For details, see **Ibid.**, pp. 265-293.
14. Stewart, Charles, and Hoss Salim, "Railroads, Politics and Regional Development in the Fertile Crescent," **Al Ab'hath**, Dec. 1961.
15. Feis, **op. cit.**, p. 329. "The loan was finally issued in Paris in April, 1914, after Turkey had reached an agreement with Greece about the islands. In compensation for this aid and for withdrawing opposition to the Bagdad Railway, railroad concession for 2,300 miles of line in Syria and Anatolia were secured. French companies were to be given rights to harbor works in three Mediterranean and two Black Sea ports. French officials were to be employed in the Turkish financial and public works services. M. Joly, a Frenchman, was made Inspector-General of Finance. The privileges of French institutions and schools, hospitals, and churches were confirmed and extended."
16. Earle, **op. cit.**, p. 53, footnote (12).
17. Feis, **op. cit.**, p. 320.

18. Until World War I, the Anatolian Railway Company was a Turkish Société Anonyme with the majority of its shares in German hands.

19. Woods, **Geographical Journal**, July 1917, **loc. cit.**, p. 35, states that "It was at the same time (in 1888), too, that the Turks first accepted the idea of providing kilometric guarantees for railways," This conflicts with Feis, **op. cit.**, p. 294, "In 1870 Baron Hirsch formed an Austro-French company to build and operate the line (network of 2,500 kilometres in European Turkey). Under the terms of his concession the company was promised a bond subsidy for construction of 14,000 francs per kilometer and guaranteed gross annual receipts over a fixed amount."

20. For detailed accounts on the Bagdad Railway, refer to footnote (2) of the first page Section II, Chapter II. Earle's thesis rests on the assumption that the Bagdad Railway was a major step in Germany's economic and political penetration of the Ottoman Empire. Chapman exposes the keen rivalries between the Foreign Powers and demonstrates how Britain, whose interests were jeopardized in the area, tried to obstruct the construction of the Bagdad line by Germany.

21. Chapman, **op. cit.**, p. 24. "Once the concession had been acquired, Siemens and Caillard worked to get British capital to participate in the railway project, but with only temporary success. In the Société du Chemin de fer Ottoman d'Anatolie, which was organized in 1889, shares amounting to £1,000,000 were taken by British bankers, and 3 seats on the board of directors of the company went to the British participants. But in 1890, when Baring Brothers, one of Britain's leading foreign investment houses, closed its doors because of the financial crisis in Argentina, the London money market became very tight.

"In the early concession of 1899, Anglo-French interests were assured 40% of the shares of the Bagdad Railway, the Turks 20% and the Germans absorbed the rest. However, since neither British nor French official consent was forthcoming, the first section of the Bagdad line was subscribed by the following concerns: 10% by the Anatolian Railway, 10% by the Turkish Government and 80% by the Deutsche Bank. Conversion of the Turkish public debt in 1903 provided the financiers with the necessary finance to build the first section of 200 kilometres between Konia and Bulgurlu."

22. Dominian, **Bulletin of the American Geographical Society**, 1915, **loc. cit.**, p. 936. "By acquiring mastery of this trunk line the Germans had succeeded in taking a first mortgage on Turkey."

23. Prothero, **Turkey in Europe**, **op. cit.**, p. 66.

24. See Appendix for the complete text of this concession. Also, Earle, **op. cit.**, pp. 77-78, gives a lengthy account of the concession.

25. Hoskins, **op. cit.**, p. 451. In addition, the following is stated in the British Handbook "Anatolia" Prothero, edit., **op. cit.**, p. 48. "In estimating the prospects of the Baghdad railway within the limits of Anatolia, a distinction must be made between the sections west of the Taurus Mountains and those beyond. From Konia to the mountains the line runs for the most part over an unproductive tableland. Here and there, it is true, it touches fertile tracts, but in general the country is naturally unsuited to agriculture. In the neighborhood of Konia itself the Germans have sought to supply the deficiencies of nature by the construction of large irrigation works, but hitherto the surplus produce of the district has been sent to Constantinople by the Anatolia railway, and the Bagdad line seems to have benefited little by the improvements. It is true that before the war the traffic receipts of the section from Konia to Bulgurlu, though not large, were steadily increasing; but it seems probable that for many years this section will be mainly important as a link between the Anatolian railway and the regions beyond the Taurus.

East of the mountains very different conditions prevail, for the line runs through the Cilician plain, which already yields rich crops of cereals and cottons, and, with the spread of modern methods of tillage and irrigation, should in the near future become one of the most flourishing districts on the Mediter ranean sea-board."

26. Dominian, **Bulletin of the American Geographical Society, 1915, loc. cit.**, p. 936. "The international character of the line became more and more pronounced between the years of 1908 and 1911. During this period a number of agreements were signed between Great Britain, France, Germany and Turkey in which a notable percentage of German interests passed over to the two rival countries, the Germans emerging out of the transaction with a bare majority."

27. Political and military reasons were responsible for choosing the overland, rather than the shorter sea route. Fear of naval attack by enemy ships had to be considered. Also, Russian demands forced an alteration of the original overland scheme.

28. Feis, **op. cit.**, p. 354. "By this convention, as a prelude to a new arrangement, the Bagdad Railway Company returned its rights to the line beyond Bagdad and the ports at Basra to the Turkish Government—under condition that their construction, if and when undertaken, should be by a Turkish company interna-

tionally owned and administered. The way was again clearly open for international negotiations."

29. Wood, Geographical Journal, loc. cit., (1917), p. 34. "As the Taurus Tunnels were pierced in Nov. 1916, it is probable that these tunnels are now open at least for good traffic."
30. For details, refer to Prothero, Turkey in Europe, op. cit., p. 68.
31. Feis, op. cit., p. 319.
32. Consult maps in various books on the O.E.
33. After World War I, the Ottoman American Development Company, comprised of American entrepreneurs, endeavored to eke out new concessions for railway development in modern Turkey. A concession was granted by the Grand National Assembly on April 9, 1923. A point of interest in this concession is the fact that the agreement carried with it mining concessions in lieu of kilometric guarantees. Unfortunately, the concessionnaires failed to live up to the agreement which had to be canceled.
34. Refer to Section B, on French Investment (Chapter II, Section II, B).
35. Dominian, Bulletin of the American Geographical Society, 1915, loc. cit., p. 938.
36. Gordon, op. cit., p. 131. "The prewar investment of foreign capital in Turkey's railway system amounted to $170,070,828.

CHAPTER III, PART I

1. Mears, op. cit., p. 222, "From a railway standpoint, Turkey, similar to China, India, and other backward countries, is greatly underdeveloped. There is nothing resembling a unified railway system in Turkey due to independent penetration by nationals of foreign countries in their desire to cultivate special spheres of influence. The sordid story of blackmail and bribery which accompanied the promotion and the operation of railways in Turkey reflects little credit on concessionaires, foreign chancellories, or Ottoman officials."
2. Earle's thesis establishes definite relationships and presents evidence to the effect that Germany had imperialistic designs on Turkey. It was not uncommon during the nineteenth century for industrial nations to colonize or act aggressively in an attempt to find markets for their manufactured products as well as for raw materials. Germany's economic penetration was not novel in itself, but the way it was applied with deft shrewdness and swiftness brought about indignant surprises from other nations.
3. Mears, op. cit., p. 216. "To discover the main interior centers of trade and communication, one cannot go far wrong in naming the capitals of the vilayets and sanjaks. Among the most prominent are Eski Shehr, Afium, Qarahisar, Konia, Adana, Angora, Amasia, Sivas, Diarbekr, Nisibin, Van, Bitlis and Kharput. Primitive conditions exist in all these localities. Their importance is due not to industrial development or commercial enterprise but rather to their situation on through travel routes. Of immeasurably less importance than the coast cities from the standpoint of foreign trade, the interior distributing points, nevertheless, are the scene of the great majority of domestic trade transactions."
4. Mears, op. cit., p. 223.
5. Fraser, op. cit., p. 25.
6. Prothero, Turkey in Europe, op. cit., p. 137. "The Compagnie des Eaux de Constantinople (Darkos Water Co.) is under French control, and the Constantinople Quay Company under France-British control, but all of Haidar Pasha, and the Compagnie des Eaux de Scutari et Haidar Pasha are German or Austro-German concerns."

7. Town in this context is to be understood in the limited sense of an Eastern town rather than of a Western town.
8. Fraser, op. cit., p. 19.
9. Fraser, op. cit., p. 19.
10. Ibid., p. 76. Also see the Section on the Social Structure in Chapter I.
11. Ibid., p. 284.
12. Refer to the British Handbooks, esp. Anatolia and Mesopotamia. Anatolia, op. cit., p. 50.
13. Prothero, Turkey in Asia, op. cit., p. 69.
14. Prothero, Turkey in Asia, op. cit., p. 69.
15. Refer to the Section on the Social Structure in Chapter I.
16. Earle, op. cit., p. 16. "Extravagant prophecies have been made regarding the role of irrigation about an agricultural renaissance in Turkey-in-Asia. A writer in the Vienna Zeit of August 31, 1901, predicted that as soon as the economic effects of irrigation and the Bagdad Railway should be fully realized, 'Anatolia, northern Syria, Mesopotamia, and Irak together will export at least as much grain as all of Russia exports today.' Dr. Rohrbach claimed that this probably would prove to be an exaggeration, but that certainly Mesopotamia would become one of the great granaries of the world."
17. Woods, Geographical Journal, 1917, loc. cit., p. 41. "The work is in the hands of a German company, which was formed in 1907 as an offshoot of the Anatolian and Bagdad Railway Companies. Its task is to bring the waters of Lakes Beyshehr and Karaviran (Soghla Geul) through the gorges of the Charshembe Chai to irrigate a large district surrounding Cumbe Station which lies about 25 miles to the south-east of Konia—if properly done some 132,000 acres of arid plain will have been effectively watered. . . . To accomplish this object more than 200,000,000 cubic yards of water will be required every year. Although even in dry seasons it has been ascertained that some 230,000,000 cubic yards of water can be obtained from the Beyshehr Lake, yet it is obvious that the expense of making the necessary canals, etc. will only be able to be recovered gradually by the Ottoman Government. This the Turks hoped to be able to do by selling portions of the land irrigated, by raising the rents upon the tenants, and by decreasing, if not altogether by doing away with, the balance to be paid on the kilometric guarantees of at least this section of the Bagdad Railway."
18. Earle, op. cit., p. 5.
19. Dominian, Bulletin of the American Geographical Society, 1915, loc cit., p. 939. "A hopeful view of the future of Turkey's econo-

mic position may be entertained by remembering that the land is still unexploited and that the resources of its soil and subsoil await the handling of Western energy. It is expected that as fine a cereal crop as can be obtained anywhere in the world will be raised in the region between Eskisheir, Angora and Konia. Five million dollars spent by Germans on irrigation at Chumra in the vicinity of the last-named city has proved conclusively that a thriving agricultural industry can be reared on the interior plateau of Asia Minor. The Cilician plain, where cotton and cereals are cultivated, contains vast tracts of swamp land which can be reclaimed. Here, too, irrigation would greatly improve cotton culture. Many of these rich soils are parts of Turkish crownlands which have been estimated by some as attaining one-tenth of the entire area of Turkey. The lands owned by Evkaf, or Ministry of Religious Foundations, also cover vast areas (as an instance of this they could point to the development of sericulture in Turkey. Under the auspices of the Ottoman Public Debt Administration, tens of thousands of dollars were expended in the reclamation of more than 130,000 acres of land and the planting thereon of over sixty million mulberry trees. As a result, the silk crop increased more than ten fold during the years of 1890-1910, with a result that there was a corresponding increase in the 10% levy (or tithe) on agricultural products in the regions affected)."

20. Blaisdell, op. cit., p. 19.

21. Of the important receipts to the Ottoman Government for the fiscal year 1911-1912, the following figures are taken from Mears, op. cit., table III, p. 399. Direct taxes: T.L. (Turkish pounds) 15,724,800 or 50.5% of the total revenue. These are subdivided into: Land taxes: T.L. 2,866,900; military exemption: T.L. 1,795,300; payments in kind: T.L. 607,400; livestock taxes: T.L. 2,106,200; tithes: T.L. 7,849,100; all other: T.L. 499,900. Stamps, fees, and others amounted to T.L. 1,437,000 or 4.6%; indirect taxes including customs: 5,514,700 or 17.7%; and monopolies on salt, tobacco, posts, telegraphs, telephones and others: 3,673,900 T.L. or 11.8%.

22. Elaborating on the specific meaning and contents of tithes, Mears, op. cit., p. 398 explains: "Instead of being one-tenth of the value of the product, as its name implies, the tithe actually amounts to 12.1 percent of the crop, 10 per cent going directly to the government, 1 per cent being devoted to the agricultural bank, 0.5 per cent to public instruction and 0.6 per cent to military armaments."

Note that the tithe in the 1911-1912 receipts of the Ottoman budget amounted to about 25% of the total revenues as indicated in footnote (1) above.

23. Prothero, Turkey in Asia, op. cit., p. 69.

24. Blaisdell discusses the role of the Public Debt Administration at length in various parts of his book. Following is just a sample of his discussion, op. cit., p. 7. "Moreover, direct benefits to the native peasantry can be traced to the cooperation of the Council with foreign railway companies and banks. In the adjudication of tithes assigned as railway guarantee, or as security for governmental loans, the agents of the P.D.A. had an 'an effective' voice in all proceedings. These employees spurred on procrastinating Government officials who were charged with auctioning of pledged tithes; the Council in Constantinople was an exacting master, and obligations to the Ottoman Bank and the Deutsche Bank had to be rigidly discharged. Thus, under ordinary circumstance, the peasants were assured a fair price for their grain, and could depend on the auctions being held at favorable moments. The operation of the railways increased the productivity of the regions traversed by assuring the natives of means of transportation for all production beyond local requirements. In 1889 the value of the tithes in the provinces traversed by the Anatolian Railway was Ltqs. (Turkish pounds) 145,378; for the year 1898 this figure was Ltqs, 215,470, while in 1909 it reached Ltqs 291,919." footnote (6) "Ltqs is the abbreviation for Livres Turques, (Turkish pounds. Normal exchange of the Turkish gold pound is Ltqs 1.10 (110 piastres) to the pound sterling, or about \$1.10."

25. Blaisdell, op. cit., p. 128.

26. With regards to the early role of the Public Debt Administration, Blaisdell, op. cit., p. 3, has this to say: "In 1888 the Ottoman Government granted to the Deutsche Bank, of Berlin, a concession for the extension to Angora of the sixty-mile railway running south from Haidar Pasha (Constantinople). The Debt accepted the responsibility of collecting for the Bank certain imperial revenues which, by the concession, had been assigned to guarantee a minimum annual return for the railway. In later years a simiar obligation was undertaken towards other progeny of the Deutsche Bank, such as further extensions of the Anatolian Railway and the Bagdad Railway. This function was assumed also for the benefit of the French-constructed Smyrna-Cassaba and Salonica Junction-Constantinople lines, and the network of French railways in Syria, which enterprises were the off-spring of the Imperial Ottoman Bank, the creation of English and French capital with the latter dominant. Thus the

Council was impartial in its willingness to undertake the administration of railway guarantees."

27. Refer to Mears, op. cit., pp. 348-349.
28. Refer to tables on p. 174.
29. Mears, op. cit., p. 335. "By analysis of the trade figures for 1914, the imports can be classified into manufactured goods 59.4 per cent, cereals 25 per cent, raw materials 7 per cent, miscellaneous 8.6 per cent; and the exports into manufactured goods 13 per cent, cereals 45 per cent, raw materials 38.4 per cent, miscellaneous 3.6 per cent."
30. See Appendix for a sample on Conventions. Also, see Earle, op. cit., p. 117.
31. Fraser, op. cit., p. 78.
32. Refer to Section on Social Structure, Chapter I.
33. Referring to Abdul Hamid's attitude on railroad transportation, Earle, op. cit., p. 20, states: "But Sultan Abdul Hamid was no less interested than foreign bondholders in the extension of railway construction in his empire. Railways could be utilized, he believed, to serve his dynastic and imperial ambitions. Effective transportation was essential to the solution of at least three vexatious political problems: first, the problem of exercising real, as well as nominal, authority over rebellious and indifferent subjects in Syria, Mesopotamia, Kurdistan, Arabia, and other outlying provinces; second, the problem of compelling these provinces, by military force if necessary, to contribute their share of blood and treasure to the defence of the empire; third, the problem of perfecting a plan of mobilization for war, on whatever form it might be necessary to conduct hostilities. The maintenance of order, the enforcement of universal military service, the collection of taxes in all provinces of the empire, and defence against foreign invasion—all of these policies would be seriously handicapped, if not paralyzed, by the absence of adequate railway communications."

    For strategic reasons, if for no other, Abdul Hamid would have especially favored the Bagdad Railway.
34. Woods, Geographical Journal, July 1917, loc. cit., p. 52.
35. Feis, op. cit., p. 317. "It was not only in response to government demands that foreign capital moved into Turkey. All organized large-scale enterprise was dependent upon it and owned by it. The Turkish banking system was entirely foreign, and foreign banks conducted the official business as well as private business. The railroad system was financed almost entirely from outside, as were irrigation and municipal public utilities. The economic development of Turkey rested in the hands of those who could

amass large capital sums and utilize the machine technique. With so incompetent a government, so unorganized a people, it was almost inevitable that the political fate of Turkey should rest in the same hands."

36. **Ibid.**, p. 320. "The French holdings of Turkish public debt and investment in Turkish enterprises exceeded that of any other country. Of the twenty-six loan emissions of the Turkish Government between 1854 and 1914, French investment in railroads exceeded half a billion francs; vast further concessions secured in 1913-14 provided for 2,300 kilometers of new construction and still larger investment. French capital controlled the Banque Imperiale Ottomane, which with its sixty-two branches, was Treasurer-General and fiscal agent for Turkey. This bank brought out most of the Turkish loans in Paris. It shared control of the Turkish Tobacco Monopoly with an Austro-German group. Through interlocking directorates it was represented on all the important French railways in Turkey, and on the Bagdad Railway. The French port companies at Constantinople and Beirut, the companies which supplied water, street-car service, and electric light to Constantinople acknowledged its interest. Working in connection with this bank and other French banks, French companies held besides numerous contracts and ventures throughout the Empire—roads, ports, docks, tramways, irrigation works, lighting and power plants. Despite Turkish friendship for Germany, it was the French investor who above all financed economic change in Turkey."

37. The subject of foreign investment in Turkey and the alternatives opened to foreign investors will be discussed further in the last chapter.

38. Earle, **op. cit.**, p. 36. "That German traders should follow German financiers into the Ottoman Empire was to be expected. The Deutsche Bank—sponsor of the Anatolian Railways—had been notably active in the promotion of German foreign commerce. From its very inception it had devoted itself energetically to the promotion of industrial and commercial activity abroad, thus carrying out the object announced in its charter of "fostering and facilitating commercial relations between Germany, other European countries, and oversea markets." By the establishment of foreign branches, by the liberal financing of import and export shipments, by the introduction of German bills of exchange in the four corners of the earth, and by other similar methods, this great bank was largely responsible for the emancipation of German traders from their former dependence upon British banking facilities. The Anatolian Railway concessions marked the

initial efforts of the Deutsche Bank at Constantinople. What it had done elsewhere it could be expected to do in the interests of German business men operating in Turkey."

39. Earle, **op. cit.**, p. 37. "The London Times of Oct. 28, 1898, contained a significant review of the status of German enterprise in the Ottoman Empire during the decade immediately preceding. Whereas ten years before, the finance and trade of Turkey were practically monopolized by France and Great Britain, the Germans were now by far the most active group in Constantinople and in Asia Minor. Hundreds of German salesmen were traveling in Turkey, vigorously pushing their wares and studiously canvassing the markets to learn the wants of the people. . . .

    Promoters, bankers, traders, engineers, munitions manufacturers, shipowners, and railway builders all were playing their parts in laying a substantial foundation for a further expansion of German economic interests in the Ottoman Empire."

40. Earle, **op. cit.**, p. 36. "In 1889, for example, a group of Hamburg entrepreneurs established the Deutsche Levante Linie, which inaugurated a direct steamship service between Hamburg, Bremen, Antwerp, and Constantinople. It was the expectation of the owners of this line that the construction of the Anatolian railways would materially increase the volume of German trade with Turkey—an expectation which was justified by subsequent developments. In 1888, the year of the original railway concession to the Deutsche Bank, exports from Germany to Turkey were valued at 11,700,000 marks; by 1893, when the line was completed to Angora, they mounted to a valuation of 40,900,000 marks, an increase of about 350%. Imports into Germany from Turkey during the same period rose from 2,300,000 marks to 16,500,000 marks, showing an increase in volume of German exports to Turkey can be attributed to the use of German materials on the Ismid-Angora railway. In any event, there was no further substantial development of this export trade between 1895 and 1900, although imports into Germany from Turkey reached the high figure of 28,900,000 marks at the close of the century."

41. Gordon, **op. cit.**, p. 62. "The list of commodities imported from Turkey well illustrates the primitive basis of the export trade of that country. American importations of agricultural products amounted to 58 per cent of the total in 1928. Owing to the continued predominance of tobacco, fruits, nuts, rugs, and carpets, the importations of which amounted to 70 per cent of the total import trade in 1928, there has been no great change in the nature of the commodities imported from Turkey since 1900."

Other imported items include undressed furs, mohair, hides, and skins, unmanufactured wool, drugs, dyes, chemicals and licorice roots etc.

42. **Ibid., p. 82.** "A division of Turkish exports to the United States for 1928 on the basis of this classification discloses the fact that 64 per cent of the commodities fell within the group classed as raw materials while 28 per cent were consumption goods. There were no imports of finished capital goods, the remaining 8 per cent comprising miscellaneous items. Further examination reveals the fact that by far the larger part of the imports were agricultural products."

American exports included breadstuffs, cotton manufactures, mineral oils, and of lesser significance, cotton goods, iron and steel products, electrical appliances and machinery, and leather manufactures. For further details check pp. 51-65.

43. Gordon, **op. cit.,** p. 45. "Looking at the total volume of trade for the period from 1862 to 1900 it is seen that with the exception of years when total figures were not available or when some unusual event affected commercial relations the figures show a comparatively steady increase reaching $7,000,000 in 1897. That general upward trend is minimized by the fact that during the last quarter of the period the general level of wholesale prices was falling. Mention also should be made of the fact that during the same period there was an upward trend in American tariff rates on commodities imported from Turkey which no doubt retarded the development of Turkish-American trade, the more so since the bulk of the commerce consisted of imports from Turkey."

CHAPTER IV

1. Much of what is said in this chapter has depended on the following books and articles. Sources on Turkish railways were previously cited. Bolino, A. C., **The Development of the American Economy,** Charles E. Merrill Books Inc., Columbus, Ohio, 1966, Chapter 6. Clapham, J. H., **An Economic History of Modern Britain,** Vol. I, Cambridge, 1930, Chapter 9; Clapham, J. H., **The Economic Development of France and Germany,** 1815-1914, Cambridge, 1921, Chapter 7; Davis, Lance E. et al. **American Economic History,** Richard D. Irwin, Homewood, Illinois, 1961, Chapter 17. Day, Clive, **Economic Development in Europe,** New York, Macmillan Co., 1942, Chapters 22-25; Dunham, Arthur Louis, **The Industrial Revolution in France,** 1815-1848. Exposition Press, New York, Chapter 4; Sherrington, L. E. R. **A hundred years of inland transport 1830-1933,** At the Chapel River Press, Andoves, England, 1834. Taylor, George Rogers, **The Economic History of the United States, 1815-60.** Vol. IV, Holt Rinehart and Winston, New York, 1962, Gerschenkron, Alexander, "Economic Backwardness in Historical Perspective," **The Progress of Underdeveloped Areas,** The University of Chicago Press, 1952; Wicker, E. R. "Railroad Investment before the Civil War," **Studies in Income and Wealth,** Vol, 24, Princeton University Press, 1960, pp. 503-546.
2. Davis, et. al. op. cit., p. 300.
3. Fraser, op. cit., p. 296. "In America and Canada exist conditions ideal to railway enterprise, for there the ages have expended themselves in fertilising the soil, while the nations of the world have combined to send their surplus people to gather the wealth lying fallow. Building a railway across the American continent is like driving a shaft into a mountain of solid gold."
4. Taylor, op. cit., p. 100, on page 101, he adds: "In so far as private capital contributed to the building of American railroads before 1860, it came from a multitude of private savers, both large and small. The primary interest of most investors lay in the indirect benefits to be gained, though as the period advanced, purchase for investment or speculation by financiers in the eastern cities and abroad began to be important."
5. Dunham, op. cit., p. 81. "During that year (1845) 118 railroads calling for an investment of £60,484,000 had been authorized in

England and bills for more than 500 additional lines with an investment of £304,000,000 had been introduced."

6. Regulation of railways, developed towards the end of the 19th century and culminated in the Railways Act of 1921 whereby a Railway Rates Tribunal was established which took from the Railway Companies as of January 1, 1928, the duty of fixing rates and fares.
7. Taylor, op. cit., p. 95.
8. Ibid., p. 88. With respect to government regulation of railways, this did not come until the 1880's. Davis, et al, op. cit., p. 310. "The Act to Regulate Commerce was passed in 1887 and established the pattern of Federal regulation that has existed to the present. The act set up the Interstate Commerce Commission, demanded reasonable rates, and prohibited personal discrimination, long and short-haul differentiations, and freight pooling."
9. For a good sample, see the Bagdad Concession Appendix D. Jastrow, op. cit., p. 94, sums up a number of conditional privileges given by the Ottoman Government: "All material imported for the construction of the road was to be free from duty, the company was to have a monopoly of kilns erected on the route for the construction of the road, to have access to all ports and to navigation on the Euphrates and Tigris and the Shatt-el-Arab (junction with Euphrates) during the operations, and the privilege of reserving to itself the right to construct and exploit ports at Bagdad, Basra and on the Persian Gulf. In return, the Turkish government was satisfied with the demand that the workmen to be employed were to be Turkish subjects and the reins manned by Turkish officials, with the exception of the highest posts which were to be held by Germans—and that everybody connected with the railway was to wear a fez. For the present railway was to be a single track, but the Turkish government would have the right as soon as the receipts reached an average of 30,000 francs per kilometre per year to demand the laying of a second track at the expense of the company."
10. Belgium offers the best example of national undertaking in railways in the 19th cenutry. See Clapham, **Economic Development of France and Germany**, op. cit., esp.
11. Dunham, op. cit., p. 66. "No continental state could treat the railroads as individual commercial enterprises for two reasons. The problem of defending the country against invasion by land was always present, and the power of the governmental bureaucracy, partly because of the need of defense, was a tradition." In referring to financial support, Dunham states, p. 69. "Funds sufficient to finance the construction of important railroads could be

obtained only by the co-operation of the government, as the only organization having the confidence of any great body of investors, and that of the great bankers of Paris and a few other centers, such as Lyons and Rouen."

12. Sherrington, op. cit., p. 41. "Prior to 1830 only fifty-one miles of railway had been opened to traffic, consisting of many small and widely scattered lines, of which the most important was the Stockton and Darlington Railway; others of very local importance were the Kilmarnock and Troon and the Monkland and Kirkintillock in Scotland."
13. Davis, et. al. op. cit., p. 304, provides a detailed table on railway mileage in the United States.
14. Bolino, op. cit., p. 167; on page 165, he states, "Besides stimulating investment and creating a demand for goods and factors, the railroad also provided a transportation service which was essential to the development of capitalism in America. Improvement in transportation generally meant a reduction in the cost to shippers and consumers, and a greater speed in transport; more important, the railroad brought transportation to areas that would not have been settled without it."
15. Gordon, op. cit., p. 132. "The fact that in 1912 it was estimated that the rich territory comprising modern Turkey yielded only one-twelfth of its potential production can be attributed in large part to the absence of transportation facilities."
16. Earle, op. cit., p. 75. "There are special and peculiar problems connected with the construction of railways in the economically backward areas of the world. In well populated regions, such as western Europe, railways have been built to accommodate existing traffics; in sparsely populated regions, such as eastern Russia and western United States, they have been constructed chiefly to create new traffic. In the economically advanced countries of the world the railway has been the result of civilization; in the backward countries it has been the outpost of civilization. A new railway in an undeveloped region is obliged at the outset to concern itself mainly with the upbuilding of the territory through which it runs, in order to assure abundant traffic for the future; during this period its receipts are rarely, if ever, adequate to meet the costs of operation. Private capital cannot be expected to assume alone the risk and burden thus involved by the public service which the railway renders during this critical time justifies the government in subsidizing the enterprise until it can become self-supporting. The granting of state subventions has been a common practice of the 19th and 20th centuries. China time and again has pledged national revenues in

support of railway construction; the Latin-American countries have been conspicuous exemplars of the same practice; more than half of the railways of Russia were constructed with government funds."

17. Referring to the first section of the Bagdad Railway, run in Oct. 1904, Fraser, op. cit., p. 51, relates: "I have been told that in the wheat season goods trains have been known to run, but they must have been few and far between, for the total traffic, both ways, in the year 1906 only amounted to 25,000 tons. The kilometric receipts averaged only 1,368 francs, giving a total for the year's working of a little over £10,000. Owing to the scarcity of population and the impossibility of expanding cultivation, there seems no likelihood of improvement in the next few years."
18. Day, op. cit., p. 489.
19. For details see Day, op. cit., p. 503.
20. Statesman's Year Book, 1901, p. 1012.

CHAPTER V

1. Just to give an example of the burden of costs to the Ottoman Government, the following excerpt is quoted from Fraser, op. cit., p. 52. It provides early estimates of costs borne by the Porte in aiding the construction and operation of the first section of the Bagdad railway from Konia to Bulgurlu. "Meantime it costs Turkey 11,000 frs per kilometer per annum to finance this concern, paid in the shape of interest at 4% on the State loan which provided the capital for construction, together with 4,500 francs per kilometer per annum for working expenses, less the trifle earned. This means 2,200,000 francs, or £88,000, plus allowance for working expenses, which, in 1906, came to £25,000. So that for the whole concern Turkey is paying £113,000 per annum."

Another illustration of payments on concessions could be provided in the following table which is taken from Prothero, Anatolia, op. cit., p. 58.

Year	Anatolian Railway		Bagdad Railway	Smyrna-Kassab Railway
	Haidar-Angora	Eskishehir-Angora	Konia-Bulgurlu	Alashehir-Afium Karahissar
	L	L	L	L
1908	116,800	119,700	23,170	146,200
1909	102,000	119,700	20,300	153,000
1910	22,300	96,400	15,250	130,000
1911	Nil	41,900	9,500	115,000
1912	Nil	Nil	Nil	123,000
1913	Nil	11,500	16,600	127,000

Note that due to improved traffic, the amounts paid for kilometric concessions had to be reduced, particularly in 1912. Yet the Ottoman Government had to continue payments on these guaranteed concessions. It is possible that the improvement in traffic conditions was of a temporary nature, due to the Balkan Wars. During this time, armies had to be raised and transported to the battle front.

2. DuVelay does not specifically say whether the amounts paid for railway concessions were in Francs, Turkish Pounds or in any other currency, but presumably they were in Francs.
3. Mears, op. cit., p. 370. "Mr. S. Bilinski, the able general manager of the National Bank of Turkey, has prepared for the writer the following statement regarding the financial benefits from Turkish railway enterprises: Many railway companies in Turkey obtained the funds necessary for building the lines by issues of debentures, the services on which were secured by a kilometric guarantee of the State, whereas the share capital was issued in payment of the concession. The net results, therefore, were that: (a) The concessionaires, who had obtained their concessions by means which were more often dubious than not, received in payment shares which they promptly converted into cash. A large part of these profits, which can be fairly regarded as ill-gotten, no doubt found their way into the pockets of palace favorites and ministerial officials, who one and all seemed to have been imbued with the spirit of the dying miser's advice to his son: "Make money—honestly if you can,—but make it." (b) The financial groups associated with the concessionaire made money. (c) The railway contractors made money. (d) The debenture holders sporadically received interest on their money. (e) The debt charges of an already more or less bankrupt country were increased by the pernicious system of kilometric guarantees, than which nothing is more calculated to prevent the progressive working of a railway line and the development of the country it is supposed to serve.
4. Feis, op. cit., p. 316.
5. Blaisdell, op. cit., p. 125.
6. Feis, op. cit., p. 51. Feis warns that these figures are mere estimates and are not very accurate. On page 52, he adds, "French financial enterprise built and operated lighthouses and docks in the waters of the Mediterranean, the Black and Red Seas, and the Persian Gulf. In the Consortium formed in 1911 to operate the transport and electricity enterprises of Constantinople, it was preponderant; the operation of gas works and construction of sewers in that city was under its direction."
7. Feis, op. cit., p. 76.
8. Gordon, op. cit., p. 131.
9. Feis, op. cit., p. 316.

10. Fraser, op. cit., p. 327.
11. Toynbee & Kirkwood, op. cit., p. 61.
12. Issawi, Charles, "Egypt since 1800: A study in lopsided development," Journal of Economic History, Vol. XXI, March 1961, No. 1, p. 6.
13. Gerschenkron, Alexander, "Economic Backwardness in Historical Perspective," The Progress of Underdeveloped Areas, The University of Chicago Press, Chicago, 1962, p. 7.
14. Feis, op. cit., p. 360.

BIBLIOGRAPHY: BOOKS, DISSERTATIONS

Bailey, Frank Edgar, **British Policy and the Turkish Reform Movement, 1826-1853,** Harvard University Press, 1942.

Birge, John Kingsley, **A Guide to Turkish Area Study,** American Council of Learned Societies, Washington, 1949.

Blaisdell, Donald C., **European Financial Control in the Ottoman Empire,** New York, Columbia University Press, 1929.

Bolino, August C., **The Development of the American Economy,** Charles E. Merrill Books Inc., Columbus, Ohio, 2nd ed. 1966.

Cameron, Rondo E., **France and the Economic Development of Europe, 1800-1914,** Princeton University Press, 1961.

Chapman, Maybelle Rebecca, **Great Britain and the Bagdad Railway 1888-1914,** Smith College Studies in History, Northampton, Mass., 1948.

Clapham, John Harold, **An Economic History of Modern Britain,** Vol. I. Cambridge, 1930.

——————, **The Economic Development of France and Germany, 1815-1914,** Cambridge, 1921.

Correa, H. M. A., **The International Controls of Public Finance,** Krukkering, M. J. Portielzie, Amsterdam, 1926.

Davey, Richard, **The Sultan and his Subjects,** London, Chatto and Windus, 1907.

Davis, Lance, E., Hughes, Jonathan R. T., & McDougall, Duncan M., **American Economic History,** Richard D. Irwin, Homewood, Illinois, 1961.

Davison, Roderic, **Reform and Westernization in the Ottoman Empire: 1855-1876.** Doctoral Dissertation, Cambridge, Massachusetts, 1942.

Day, Clive, **Economic Development in Europe,** New York, Macmillan Co., 1942.

Dunham, Arthur Louis, **The Industrial Revolution in France 1815-1848,** Exposition Press, New York, 1955.

DuValay, A., Essai sur l'Histoire Financière de la Turquie (depuis le régne du Sultan Mahmoud II jusqu'a nos jours), Paris, Arthur Rousseau, Editeur, 14, Rue Soufflet, Et Rue Toullier, 13-1903.

Earle, Edward M., **Turkey, the Great Powers, and the Bagdad Railway,** New York, Macmillan Co., 1928.

Emin, Ahmed, **The Development of Modern Turkey as measured by its Press,** New York, Columbia Press, 1914.

Everseley, Lord George J. S., **The Turkish Empire, its Growth and Decay,** T. F. Unwin Ltd. 1918.

Feis, Herbert, **Europe the World's Banker 1870-1914**, New Haven, Yale University Press, 1930.
Fraser, David, **The Short Cut to India.** The record of a journey along the route of the Baghdad Railway. Second Impression, William Blackwood and Sons, Edinburgh and London, 1909.
Gibb, H. A. R. and Bowen, H., **Islamic Society and the West**, London, Oxford University Press, Vols. I & II, 1950 and 1957 respectively.
Gordon, Leland James, **American Relations with Turkey, 1830-1930, An Economic Interpretation**, University of Pennsylvania Press, London, H. Milford, Oxford University Press, 1932.
Hoskins, Halford Lancaster, **British Routes to India.** A thesis in History. University of Pennsylvania, Philadelphia, 1928, Longmans, Green & Co., New York.
Issawi, Charles, **The Economic History of the Middle East, 1800-1914.** The University of Chicago Press, 1966.
Jastrow, Morris, **The War and the Baghdad Railway**, Second Impression, Philadelphia and London; J. B. Lippincott Co., 1918.
Lengyel, Emil, **Turkey**, Random House, New York, 1941.
Lewis, Bernard, **The Arabs in History**, New York, Harper and Brothers, 1960.
——————, **The Emergence of Modern Turkey**, Oxford University Press, London, 1961.
Issawi, Charles, **The Economic History of the Middle East, 1800-1914**, The University of Chicago Press, 1966.
Lewis, W. Arthur, **The Theory of Economic Growth**, Richard D. Irwin Inc., Homewood, Illinois, 1955.
Mardin, Serif, **The Genesis of Young Ottoman Thought**, Princeton University Press, 1961.
Mears, Elliot Grinnell, **Modern Turkey**, New York, Macmillan Co., 1924.
Michelsen, Edward H., **The Ottoman Empire and Its Resources**, Second Edition, London, William Spooner, 379, Strand, 1854.
Miller, William, **The Ottoman Empire and its Successors 1801-1927**, Cambridge University Press, 1936, 4th edition.
Milikan, Max F. & Blackmer, Donald L. M., **The Emerging Nations**, Massachusetts Institute of Technology, 1961.
Morawitz, Charles, **Les Finances de la Turquie**, Paris, 1902.
Patrick, Mary Mills, **Under Five Sultans**, New York, Central Co., 1929.
Pears, Sir Edwin, **Life of Abdul Hamid**, New York, Henry Holt and Co., 1917.
Phillips, M., **A History of Turkey from Empire to Republic**, George Allen and Unwin, Ltd., 1956.
Ramsaur Jr., Ernest E., **The Young Turks—Prelude to the Revolu-**

tion of 1908, Princeton University Press, Princeton, New Jersey, 1957.

Sherrington, C. E. R., **A Hundred Years of Inland Transportation 1830-1933**, Duckworth, 3, Henrietta St. W.C. 2, 1934. (At the Chapel River Press, Andoves Hauts).

Taylor, George Rogers, **The Economic History of the United States 1815-1860**, Vol. IV, Holt, Rinehart and Winston, New York, August 1962.

Toynbee, Arnold J. & Kirkwood, Kenneth P., **Turkey**, New York, Charles Scribner's Sons, 1927.

Vaka, Demetra, **Haremlek**, Houghton Mifflin Co., Boston and New York, 1909.

Waugh, Sir Telford, **Turkey, Yesterday, Today and Tomorrow**, Chapman and Hall's, 1930.

Webster, Sir Charles Kingsley, **The Foreign Policy of Palmerston 1830-1841**, Vols. I & II, London, G. Bell & Sons, Ltd., 1951.

White, Wilbur W., **The Process of Change in the Ottoman Empire**, The University of Chicago Press, Chicago, Illinois, 1937.

Urquhart, David, **Turkey and its Resources**, London, Saunders and Otley, 1833.

ARTICLES, PERIODICALS

Dominian, Leon, "The Peoples of Northern and Central Asiatic Turkey," **Bulletin of the American Geographical Society**, Vol. XLVII, No. 11, (1915), pp. 832-871.

Dominian, Leon, "Railroads in Turkey," **Bulletin of the American Geographical Society**, Vol. XLVII, No. 12 (Dec. 1915), pp. 934-944.

Gerschenkron, Alexander, "Economic Backwardness in Historical Perspective," **The Progress of Underdeveloped Areas**, The University of Chicago Press, 1952.

Hershlag, Z. Y., "Turkey, Achievements and Failures in the Policy of Economic Development during the Inter-War Period, 1919-1939," **Kyklos**, Vol. VII, (1954).

Issawi, Charles, "Egypt since 1800: A Study in Lop-Sided Development," **Journal of Economic History**, Vol. XXI, No. 1, (March 1961).

Karal, Enver Ziya, "Historiography in Turkey Today," **Middle Eastern Affairs**, Vol. X, No. 10, (Oct. 1959).

Newcombe, S. F. & Greig, J. P. S., "The Bagdad Railway," **Geographical Journal**, Vol. 44, (1914), pp. 577-580.

Nicholls, William, "Domestic Trade in an Underdeveloped Country—

Turkey," **Journal of Political Economy**, Vol. LIX, No. 4, (Dec. 1951).

Stewart, Charles F. and Salim, Hoss, "Railroads, Politics and Regional Development in the Fertile Crescent," **Al Ab'hath**, (Dec. 1961).

Wicker, E. R., "Railroad Investment before the Civil War," **Studies in Income and Wealth**, Vol. 24, Princeton University Press, (1960), pp. 502-546.

Woods, H. Charles, "Communications in the Balkan," **Geographical Journal**, Vol. XLVII, No. 4, (April 1916), pp. 265-293.

—————, "The Baghdad Railway and its Tributaries," **Geographical Journal**, Vol. L, July 1917, pp. 32-56.

ENCYCLOPEDIAS, HANDBOOKS, YEAR-BOOKS, etc.

Encyclopedia Britannica, William Benton, Publisher, Chicago, London, Toronto, (1961), "Capitulations," pp. 813-814, vol. 4; "Janissaries," pp. 890-891, vol. 12; "Turkey,' pp. 588-617, vol. 22.

Encyclopedia of Islam, Edited by M. Th. Houtsma, H. A. R. Gibb, et. al. Leyden, Late E. J. Brill Ltd. London, "Tanzimat," pp. 656-660; "Turks," pp. 900-972.

Anatolia, Handbook prepared under the Historical Section of the Foreign Office No. 59, London. Published by H. M. Stationery Office, G. W. Prothero, General Editor and formerly Director of the Historical Section, 1920.

Mesopotamia, Same as above, No. 63.

Turkey in Asia, Same as above No. 58.

Turkey in Europe, Same as above No. 16.

Statesman's Year-Book, 1864-1921, Macmillan and Co., Ltd. St. Martin's St. London.

APPENDIX A

Ottoman Sultans in the 19th and 20th centuries.

Selim III	1789-1808
Mahmud II	1808-1839
Abdul Mejid	1839-1861
Abdul Aziz	1861-1876
Murad	August 1876
Abdul Hamid II	1876-1908
Mohammed V	1908-1918
Mohammed VI	1918-1922

Following are significant and interesting comments on each one of the above Sultans:

Miller, op. cit., p. 18; "Selim III, who at this time sat on the throne, was, it is true, a reforming Sultan, anxious to raise his empire from its declining state, and willing to take western nations as his model. He made, for a moment, a clean sweep of the Bulgarian and Macedonian brigands and the Aegean pirates, repaired the ruinous fortresses on his frontiers and employed French shipbuilders to construct men-of-war. But, like most autocrats, he was powerless to change a whole system of misgovernment with a stroke of his pen."

Davey, Richard, The Sultan and His Subjects, London, Chatto and Windus, 1907, "Mahmud, who was a pupil of Selim III, was a man of considerable ability, if not of absolute genius. Physically, he was according to Lord Stratford de Redcliffe, of diminutive stature. His head was large and his features regular and handsome. He had astonishingly expressive eyes and a wonderfully powerful voice."

Ramsaur, op. cit., p. 3, "The profligate and sensuous Sultan Abdul Aziz (1861-76), who allowed the forms undertaken by his predecessor, Abdul Mejid (1839-61), to remain a dead letter and had no interest in anything but the indulgence of his own fancies."

Lord Eversley, op. cit., p. 311, "He was the first sultan to fall into the hands of money lenders of Western Europe. Great sums were borrowed ostensibly for the war with Russia. But the larger part of them were expended by Abdul Medjid in wild extravagance, in gratifying the caprices of the multitudes of women in his harem, in building palaces, and in satisfying the demands of corrupt ministers. On the occasion of the marriage of one of his daughters with the son of a Grand Vizier he spent forty millions of francs on her trousseau and in fêtes."

Ramsaur, op. cit., p. 11, "Abdul Hamid was engrossed with the idea of maintaining himself on the throne. His whole reign was devoted to that end. The notorious espionage system which made every man a spy on his neighbor, the policy of exiling anyone who disagreed with him, the practice of allowing his servants to enrich themselves at public expense so that they would remain faithful to him; in short, the entire Hamidian system had but one aim: the security of the Sultan himself.

Abdul Hamid has been described as a man of consummate skill in the game of playing off opposing forces, internal and external, against one another."

Miller, op. cit., p. 368, "The British fleet arrived in Besik Bay; and on May 29 the new Grand Vizier and his confederates, having obtained a fetwah from the Sheik-ul-Islam authorising the deposition of Abdul Aziz on the ground of his incapacity and extravagance, declared the throne vacant and on the following day proclaimed his nephew Sultan under the title of Murad V. . . The removal of his uncle did not, however, long confirm Murad on the throne. The tragedy of his sudden elevation to power affected a mind naturally feeble; the National party soon recognized that he was not the man to direct the fortunes of the empire in a time of dire distress. On August 31 he was deposed in his turn, and his brother Abdul Hamid II took his place."

Miller, op. cit., p. 482, writes on Mohammed V, "The new Sultan was a mere puppet in the hands of the Committee." [The Committee was formed at Geneva in 1891, under the title of Union and Progress, and proclaimed Mohammed V as the new Sultan, after the deposition of his brother Abdul Hamid]. "Of the world he could know little, for he had been confined by his brother within the gilded cage of his palace, and he is said to have declared 'that he had not read any newspaper for twenty years.' "

APPENDIX B

BUDGETS OF THE OTTOMAN EMPIRE, 1909-10 TO 1914-15*
Budget as presented to the Chamber of Deputies
(in Turkish pounds)

	Estimated Receipts	Estimated Expenditures	Estimated Deficits
1909-10	25,078,962	30,539,545	5,460,583
1910-11	29,183,418	35,994,587	6,811,169
1911-12	31,645,708	41,161,729	9,516,021
1912-13	33,682,475	36,691,366	3,208,891
1913-14	33,682,475	36,691,366	3,208,891
1914-15	36,004,213	36,054,605	1,050,392
	Actual Receipts	**Actual Expenditures**	**Actual Deficits**
1911-12	27,269,751	29,908,282	2,638,531
1912-13	27,544,759	38,919,877	10,375,118
1913-14	29,201,865	35,329,950	6,128,085
1914-15	24,739,164	57,841,339	33,102,175

*The table was prepared from figures courteously furnished by the Ottoman Public Debt. (1)

---

(1) Mears, op. cit., p. 390, Chapter XVII, "The Public Treasury," by William Wilson Cumberland.

APPENDIX C

Finances

The Finances of Turkey, during the last four years, have been in a very low condition. The cause of the embarrassment may chiefly be found in the excessive number of the standing army, introduced and maintained by the previous administration, under a faulty system.

The Budget of the Revenue for 1852 was as follows:

	Piastres		£
Tithes	220,000,000	or	2,200,000
Land taxes	200,000,000		2,000,000
Poll tax	40,000,000		400,000
Customs	86,000,000		860,000
Indirect taxes	150,000,000		1,500,000
Tribute of Egypt	30,000,000		300,000
of Wallachia	2,000,000		20,000
of Serbia	2,000,000		20,000
of Moldavia	1,000,000		10,000
Total	731,000,000		7,310,000

Explanations pp. 174, 175.
Expenditure Budget.

	Piastres	£
Civil list of the Sultan	75,000,000	750,000
Do. of the Sultana-Mother and the Princesses	8,400,000	84,000
Army	300,000,000	3,000,000
Navy	37,500,000	375,000
Ordnance	30,000,000	300,000
Pay of the functionaries	195,000,000	1,950,000
Foreign department	10,000,000	100,000
Public Works	10,000,000	100,000
Pious and Charitable Institutions	12,500,000	125,000
Interest of Treasury bonds (6 per cent)	9,000,000	90,000
Life annuities (Sohim)	4,000,000	40,000
Do. of the former possessors of fiefs	40,000,000	400,000
Total	731,400,000	7,314,000

Source: Michelsen, op. cit., p. 173.

APPENDIX D

Chapman, op. cit., Appendix, pp. 212-213.
Article 35 of Bagdad Railway Convention of March 5, 1903
Article 30 of Cahier des Charges (Specification) of Imperial Ottoman Railway Company
Article 35 . . . Bagdad Railway Convention of March 5, 1903.

The Imperial Government guarantee to the concessionaires an annuity of 11,000 fr. per kilometre constructed and worked, and also a contract sum of 4,500 fr. per annum working expenses in respect of each kilometre worked.

This annuity of 11,000 fr. shall be met by an Ottoman State loan bearing interest at 4 per cent, with a sinking fund of 0.087538 per cent, redeemable during the period of the concession. Consequently the concessionaires will be entitled to a nominal sum of 269,110 fr. 65 c. of this State loan for each kilometre constructed and opened to traffic, and the concessionaires shall be debarred from demanding other amounts on this head from the Imperial Ottoman Government.

The total nominal of Government bonds accruing to the concessionaires by the terms of the foregoing arrangement on the signature of each special convention for each section; but the concessionaires shall make good to the Imperial Ottoman Government the sums which the latter have paid during the period of construction for the service of the bonds issued to the concessionaires, viz., till the date on which each section of the railway is provisionally accepted. These sums shall be placed by the concessionaires in the hands of Public Debt for the account of the Imperial Ottoman Government.

The Imperial Government reserve the right of modifying at any moment the system of payment of the kilometric annuity of 11,000 fr. fixed in the first paragraph of the present article, after redemption of the bonds issued in respect of the said annuity.

As soon as the growth of the traffic and receipts and the financial situation permit the issue by the concessionaires themselves of bonds of their own to replace the Government bonds which have been issued to them by the Imperial Government, the concessionaires shall come to an agreement with the Imperial Government for the purpose of carrying out this arrangement.

For the first section of 200 kilometres, beyond Konia the face value of the bonds to be issued by the Imperial Ottoman Government to the concessionaires is fixed at 54,000,000 fr. But as soon as this section is finally accepted and the length of the completed line is fixed, the exact nominal value of the bonds accruing to the concessionaires for that section shall be calculated at the rate of 269,110 fr. 65 c. per kilometre. Any surplus over this nominal amount shall be calculated at the issue price, plus interest at 4 per cent accrued up to the date of payment, and the sum thus ascertained shall be paid in cash by the concessionaires into the Imperial Treasury. The calculation shall be made at a minimum of 81½ per cent.

The Ottoman Anatolian Railway Company guarantees to the Imperial Ottoman Government the construction of the aforesaid first section of 200 kilometres, until the work of this section is completed.

In the event of the Imperial Ottoman Government deeming it necessary, they may also require the Ottoman Anatolian Railway Company to guarantee other sections, and the Ottoman Anatolian Railway Company shall have the right so to do.

The contract sum of 4,500 fr. per annum for working expenses in respect of each kilometre opened to traffic will be guaranteed to the concessionaires by a special convention for each section simultaneously with the convention regulating the annuity of 11,000 fr.

As regards the first section of 200 kilometres, beyond Konia, the above-mentioned contract sum of 4,500 fr. per kilometre per annum is secured to the concessionaires on the surplus of the guarantees already assigned to the lines of the Ottoman Anatolian Railway Company.

The service of the Government bonds which are to be issued for the aforesaid kilometric annuity of 11,000 fr. shall be secured on the special appropriations agreed on with the Imperial Government before work is begun on each section.

The Imperial Ottoman Bagdad Railway Company, on its part, further pledges, irrevocably and inalienably, to the holders of the said bonds the line from Konia to the Person Gulf [Probably Persian Gulf], and its branches with their rolling stock. Similarly, and for the same purpose, it assigns its share in the receipts from this line after payment of the working expenses, but the bondholders shall not be entitled to intervene in the administration of the company.

The aforesaid share of the receipts, after deducting working expenses—both the said share and the amount of expenses to be determined by the company's books—shall be paid annually, if need be, by the company to the Administration of the Ottoman Public Debt for the service of the bonds. The Imperial Ottoman Government shall refund to the company any sums that the latter may have supplied under this head for the service of the bonds issued. The Imperial Ottoman Government further assign, irrevocably and inalienably, to the holders of the aforementioned Government bonds their share of the gross receipts of the said line.

If the gross kilometric receipts of the line exceed 4,500 fr. but do not exceed 10,000 fr., the surplus above 4,500 frs. shall belong entirely to the Government.

214. (Continued) If the gross kilometric receipts exceed 10,000 fr., the portion up to 10,000 fr. being always divided as stated above, 60 per cent of the surplus over and above the 10,000 fr. shall pass to the Imperial Government, and 40 per cent to the Company.

It is agreed that if the gross kilometric receipts do not reach 4,500 fr. the sum required to make good the deficiency in this amount shall be paid to the concessionaires by the Government at the same time as the annuity of 11,000 fr. from the special assignments to be agreed on between the Imperial Government and the concessionaires before the fulfillment by the concessionaires of the clauses of the present convention relative to each section.

The above assignments shall be collected and paid through the agency of the Administration of the Ottoman Public Debt.

As regards the Government bonds to be issued for the construction of the different sections of the railway, the receipts accruing to the Imperial Government shall be pooled in such a manner that the amount available shall be assigned to the whole of the said bonds in proportion to the original nominal value of each issue.

Immediately after the payment of the coupons and the sinking fund of the Government bonds issued, the surplus of the receipts accruing to the Imperial Ottoman Government shall be paid to the latter annually after the completion of the formalities provided for by article 40 of the present convention.

Article 30; Cahier Des Charges of Imperial Ottoman Bagdad Railway Company.

The concessionaires are obliged to run daily at least one mixed train in each direction.

Besides this mixed train, the company shall run at least one through express train a week between Haidar-Pasha and Aleppo and vice versa.

This direct express train shall run on at least every fortnight to the Persian Gulf and vice versa.

The average speed of this train on the railway which forms the subject of the present convention shall be not less than 45 kilometres an hour, including stops, during the first five years from the opening to traffic of the whole of the main line.

On the expiration of those five years, the average speed of this direct train, including stops, shall be not less than 60 kilometres.

In addition to this, should the importance of the traffic prove the necessity for it, the company shall run through trains, comprising first and second class carriages, the average speed of which, between Haidar-Pasha and the Persian Gulf, and vice versa, shall be not less than 40 kilometres an hour.

APPENDIX E

A sample of different spelling for the same words:

Afium, Afiun
Alishehr, Alashehir, Aleshehr
Angora, Ankara
Basra, Bussora
Beirut, Beyrout, Beyrouth
Cassaba, Kassaba
Dede Agatch, Dedeagatch
Kara-Hissar, Karachisar, Qarahisar
Kuchuk Kainarja, Kutchouk Kainardji
Mahmud, Mahmoud
Moslem, Muslim; Mohammedan, Mahometan, Mehemet, Mohammed, Mohammad
Murad, Murat
Raya, Rayah
Rumili, Rumeli; Rumelia, Roumelia
Salonica, Salonika, Saloniki
Sea of Marmara, Sea of Marmora
Sheik'ul-Islam, Sheikhul-Islam, Seikul-Islam
Sheriat, Seriat

GLOSSARY

Firman, Ferman: A mere delegation of imperial authority to a minister.

Hatt, Hatti: A proclamation or a decree by the Sultan, such as the **Hatti Sherif of Gülhane** and the **Hatti Humayun.** These proclamations were two of the most important since each one was preceded by a line in the Sultan's handwriting saying: 'Let it be done as follows.' Furthermore, a **Hatt** is a mere emanation of human authority as distinguished from the fundamental laws of the Koran and the Hadith.

Irade, Imperial irade: A rescript expressing the sovereign will; a permission rather than a command; a special sanction from on high (ruling principle of the Turkish Empire).

Millet: 'Nation,' as used by the new Ottoman writers after the middle of the 19th century. Often and till the early part of the 20th century, **Millet** referred to a community or a religious group within the Ottoman Empire, organized for administrative purposes under its own leaders.

Raya, rayah, 'cattle': Terms referring to non-Muslim minorities in the Ottoman Empire, literally, 'cattle in pasture.'

Sheik'ul-Islam: Head of the Muslim Church, appointed by the Sultan with the concurrency of the Ulema.

Sublime Porte, Porte: Ministry of Foreign Affairs, known in Europe as the Ottoman Government, the "Glorious Government." The highest officials of state, such as the Grand Vizier's office, the Foreign Office with its secretariat and Terjuman Odasi, the Council of State and the Grand Council of Justice had their offices in that great building of yellow and rose plaster, called the Sublime Porte.

Tanzimat: Reforms from 1839-1877. Sometimes, it is used synonymously with the **Hatti-Sherif of Gülhane** of 1839.

Ulema, Ulemamen: Learned men, particularly in Islamic religious matters; a body comprising the clergy and chief functionaries of the law.

Vilayet, Elayet: Province, departement (department).

